GUESS WHO?!
THE SEARCH FOR YOUR TRUE IDENTITY

DR. NINA BARATIAK

The Present-Day Truth Series
Volume 1

1

TABLE OF CONTENTS

Dedication   5

Preface   7

Chapter 1 Let My People Go!   9

Chapter 2 There Will Be A Form!   23

Chapter 3 Are You The Sibling Or The Spouse?!   44

Chapter 4 God's Lost and Found!   69

Chapter 5 Thank God For Barnabas!   81

Chapter 6 The Sword Of The Lord And Of Gideon!   97

Chapter 7 Guess Who?!   121

Chapter 8 I Did It On Purpose!   134

Epilogue   147

Author's Biography   149

DEDICATION

This is dedicated to my husband of 39 years, John Baratiak. It has been his complete acceptance of me that has truly set me free.

To my daughter, Danielle Naler, who without her wisdom, grace and talent I wouldn't have been able to finish this book.

To my dear friend, Cassandra Pritchard, who has without question always believed in me and rooted me on.

To my dear friend, Kathi Shaw, who has given me endless encouragement to finish this book and who has stood by and cheered me on.

To my dear friend and business partner, Ross Harris, who has accepted me and supported me throughout this entire process.

To all of my great examples in the Kingdom who have been themselves and shined forth their uniqueness I am forever grateful for you.

PREFACE

I'm truly excited to be finished with this book and finally able to share it with you. This book is a revelation that the Lord sovereignly birthed in me over the course of many years. It is a life message. I believe it is a prophetic word to His people in this hour. I pray for each of you, my readers. I sense in the Spirit that a great transformation can take place as you read this book. As we delve into the Word, I believe that the Lord will reveal truths to you in order to affect change for a lifetime. The Lord would say for you to grab hold of all the insights He shows you as you embark on the search for your true identity!

I've organized this book like a journey that we take together. We'll go from one destination to the next. Every aspect of the journey will form a part of the picture: what God has to say about your true identity. This message has been stirring in me for years. I don't know how it's going to unfold within you, but I'm thrilled to have you join me as we explore who you are and what your God-given identity really is.

It sounds so simple. Really? Do we need a whole book about that? Isn't it enough to come out with a few scriptures? No; even though it's a simple idea, mistaken identity is a treacherous trap. Whatever your age right now, having misconceptions about your identity can impact you negatively for the rest of your life. You can be serving in the church, have a ministry, or even be the pastor of a church, but if you don't truly know who God has created you to be, a distortion is created.

I believe that a great release is coming for God's people to be who we are meant to be! A great release is coming for each one of us in the Body of Christ to become who we are intended to be!

This book is about YOU and who YOU really are. Each of us must have a revelation about who we are truly created to be – our true identity in Christ. In God's Word, we will discover how God designed each one of us. We will explore the things that often distort our identity and prevent us from realizing our full potential and destiny. At the conclusion of each chapter, I have included a few questions for you to ponder. I encourage you to journal your answers and allow God the time and space to speak to you. I pray that He will reveal truths to you about how He uniquely designed you and what He has for you to accomplish.

In this hour, we can't waste our time trying to be someone other than ourselves. You are a unique creation, and you have a unique testimony. You are meant to have a unique impact. There is a power in your uniqueness!

I want to pray with you as you begin this book:

> *Lord, I pray for your Holy Spirit to come and lead each one of us in all truth. Lord, I ask for each one reading this book: the ones whom You have drawn to the Kingdom for such a time as this. Let each one reading be filled with the purposes of God in their life. Let them have clarity - like eyeglasses that come on them. Let each one see it and understand it and run with it, Lord. As Your scripture says, "Write the vision, make it plain, that they who see it might run with it." Lord, I pray that You will make it very clear. In Jesus' name, Amen.*

CHAPTER 1

Let My People Go!

Have you ever felt forced into being someone who you aren't or forced to act in a way that isn't authentic to who you are because of people's expectations of you? Perhaps, because of the atmosphere you find yourself in, you have not been able to express the real you. I know that used to be the case for me.

I have an unique background. Born in Los Angeles, California, I was brought up in a Jewish home. My dad was an artist, and my mom was a scientist. My parents had eclectic and artistic friends, creating an uncommon environment in our home. My dad was two decades older than my mom and quite elderly when I was born. I felt different on many levels.

When I went away to college, I was 17 years old, and it would seem that I chose the university randomly. I didn't know a soul there. I still have no idea why I selected that particular school. I grew up around Jewish people; I had Jewish friends and Jewish people at my high school. The Jewish culture was all I ever knew. To that point in my life, I had been in a micro world. When I landed in the new environment at the university, it was as if I had arrived in "Protestant Land." Everybody was the same. But one of these things was not like the others! It was challenging for me to be in such an unfamiliar atmosphere; I felt the urgency to conform, or else, I felt, I'd never fit in.

On the very night that I moved into the dorms at the university, I picked up a Bible and began to read the Book of Hebrews. I had never owned a Bible of my own, and I happened to borrow one that belonged to someone I met that same night at a party. Miraculously, the Holy Spirit showed up, and I began shaking on the bed. Sovereignly, I knew! The One whom we, as a Jewish family, were not welcome to discuss - is God! I was profoundly moved at the truth about Jesus, and yet I felt tortured. I believed, falsely, that, as a Jewish person, I could not receive Him.

After several weeks of wrestling with the Truth, I came to understand that Jesus did come for the Jewish people, as well as for the Gentiles. Long (and supernatural!) story short, I finally accepted Jesus on Halloween night in Los Angeles, on my way to a party! That's just how I roll!

Interestingly, God had placed many "born-again" people in my dorm. I now lived with and amongst Christians. I, though, was in culture shock. "Protestant Land" was alien to me, and I felt like an outsider of a clique. All the young ladies wore Gunne Sax dresses. For those of you who don't remember, they were high-collared, flowery dresses with lace details. The were very sweet-looking. You have to understand, I wore army boots, I had wild, crazy hair, and I wore fatigues and overalls. I was unusual, and I looked unusual. The Christians I met all looked so sweet and normal, wearing these floral dresses. I began to think, "Well, I've got to conform. This must be what a Christian looks like."

So, I began to change my natural style because I thought, "This is what it's going to take. Nobody will like me if they know who I really am." It took decades for me to get over that way of thinking. It took me less time to get out of those Gunne Sax dresses - praise God! - but it took years to fully appreciate that God made me unique. He created me to look different and act different...because He wanted me to be different.

A Funny Dream!

I want to tell you how this book got its title. It came from a very humorous dream I had many years ago, working as a Real Estate agent. When I woke up from the dream and remembered it, I started laughing out loud! Of course, as a realtor, part of the job is advertising yourself, so that people will choose to have you help them buy or sell a home. In the dream, I had created a brand-new advertising campaign for my Real Estate business. The ad had my photo, but, instead of having my name underneath, it just said "Guess Who?!" In the dream, I thought this was brilliant! I thought that people would see it and absolutely want to use me as their agent. When I woke up, I initially remembered feeling this was a great idea. Soon after, as I began to reflect on it, I started laughing! I realized that it was the worst idea for my business because no one would know who I was! The whole point in real estate advertising is to have people know and become familiar with your name. In a way, our lives in Christ are the same. We have to know who we are, or people will define us on their own terms. We can't leave ourselves vulnerable to having other people decide who we should be. Instead, we need to have a God-birthed vision of ourselves that we can walk out carefully and purposefully.

When you think about the Scriptures, they are all connected with similar themes. There's nothing I like better than discussing the Bible in its entirety, because these messages emerge. There's not one little random story over here and another peculiar narrative over here. No! It's all the same message.

Any time I teach out of the Old Testament, I like to bring in 1 Corinthians 10:11.

1 Corinthians 10:11 *Now all these things happened to them as examples, and they were written for our admonition, upon whom the ends of the ages have come.*

A lot of Christians consider the Old Testament to be interesting and historical, but they take all of their spiritual lessons from the New Testament. However, 1 Corinthians tells us something quite different. It's talking about everything that happened to Abraham, to Moses, to Israel . . . Everything you read about in the Old Testament, it says, happened to them for examples. The events described in the Old Testament are historically accurate. They truly took place, but, they are also "written for our admonition." There are important lessons to learn from these stories that we need to glean now. We could have learned them all eventually in heaven, but instead, God intends for us to understand them and apply key truths and principles on Earth.

When we look at the Old Testament, we go back to the questions of "Who are the people of God?" and "What does it mean to be a person of God?" To answer these, we need to look at the lives of Abraham, Isaac, and Jacob. Through these patriarchs, the Lord formed a people called Israel. In fact, Jacob's name was changed to Israel. We discover in the Scriptures that the lineage created through them was not the end, but rather, it was the beginning of their story. In Genesis 12, when God spoke to Abraham, He said, "Leave Ur, and you're going to be looking for a city whose builder and maker is God." He did not mean that to be the end. It's the beginning. It's also the beginning of our story.

Later in Israel's story, we meet Moses. The Lord sends Moses to set His people free from the oppression of Egypt. Notice that they were already His people: the descendants of Abraham, Isaac and Jacob. In the same way, I believe the Lord has a new level of freedom for us in this hour. Moses is a type (a picture) to us of Jesus, and I believe that Jesus and Moses have the same message: there is a freedom to be who He has created us to be! Before that freedom comes, we must be set free from all false perceptions of ourselves, as well as bondages that have held us back.

Let's look at this in Exodus 3:7-8.

Exodus 3:7 *And the Lord said: "I have surely seen the oppression of My people who are in Egypt, and have heard their cry because of their taskmasters, for I know their sorrows."*

Isn't that us? Aren't we His people, but we still live in Egypt? We aren't in heaven yet. Things aren't perfect. I believe prophetically that some who are reading this have been derailed and have taken some wrong turns. Why is that? It's because we live in Egypt. We're not free of everything yet....but, freedom is on its way! The Scripture continues and says, "I have surely seen the oppression of My people who are in Egypt, and have heard their cry because of their taskmasters, for I know their sorrows."

Exodus 3:8 *So I have come down to deliver them out of the hand of the Egyptians, and to bring them up from that land to a good and large land, to a land flowing with milk and honey, to the place of the Canaanites and the Hittites and the Amorites and the Perizzites and the Hivites and the Jebusites.*

I love the phrase, *"So I have come down."* Doesn't this sound like John 1:14 that Jesus was made flesh and dwelt among us? And doesn't this sound like the Book of Hebrews? He was in all ways tempted like we are. He ever lives to give intercession for us. He's touched with the feeling of our infirmities. Here is our Lord "previewed" in Exodus 3. He says, "I know their sorrows ... " Doesn't it say about Jesus that He was a man acquainted with grief, that He understood our sorrows?

The verse goes on and says that He has something really amazing in store for us ... but wait! What?! There's a challenge - it's occupied! The land was occupied by enemies! God is bringing us out from where we've been, and He says, "I've got something really great for you, but right now it's occupied by all sorts and varieties of enemies." There's not just one kind of enemy there. No! There's this, and then there's that, and there's going to be these, and this is going to happen ... There are Canaanites, Hittites, Amorites, Perizzites, Hivites and Jebusites!

Let My People Go!

Exodus 5:1 *Afterward Moses and Aaron went in and told Pharaoh, "Thus says the Lord God of Israel: 'Let My people go, that they may hold a feast to Me in the wilderness.'"*

In this hour, I believe it's the cry of the Holy Spirit for a great freedom to come on God's people. The day we are living in is the great day of prophetic fulfillment! That's why it's so exciting to look at these Old Testament stories! When we delve into the Word, our perspective can be, "What does this mean, Lord? What admonition are You bringing to me today?"

There is a release for God's people in this hour, just like the story in Exodus so powerfully demonstrates. It's not only going to break people free from bondage; it's going to bring them into the land that God has promised them. What's another word for that? Your land is your destiny, your purpose, your true identity.

God wants to bring you into your destiny, but first, there are some enemies that need to be displaced from our God-given land. We're not going to simply waltz in and take the whole thing. No, it's a fight! Right? The children of Israel had Moses, but we have Jesus. What does it say about that in Hebrew 3:1-6?

Hebrews 3:1-6 *Therefore, holy brethren, partakers of the heavenly calling, consider the Apostle and High Priest of our confession, Christ Jesus, who was faithful to Him who appointed Him, as Moses also was faithful in all His house. For this One has been counted worthy of more glory than Moses, inasmuch as He who built the house has more honor than the house. For every house is built by someone, but He who built all things is God. And Moses indeed was faithful in all His house as a servant, for a testimony of those things which would be spoken afterward, but Christ as a Son over His own house, whose house we are if we hold fast the confidence and the rejoicing of the hope firm to the end.*

In other words, the Lord created Moses. We can look at what Moses did in the book of Exodus - it's great, and it's amazing, and it's mighty - but it is written for our admonition. It all happened, but it's written for our admonition. Why? It's God who created the whole scenario. It's God who created Moses. It's God who called Moses. It's God who went with Moses. Moses himself said, "I'm not going anywhere, except that You're going with me."

Moses brought Israel out, but Jesus is bringing each one of us out. In my spirit, I prophetically hear a great roar that's going to come. God is imparting strength and courage for that which He has called you to do. We cannot be those who are say, "Let's just do things the way they've always been done ... "
No.

The thing that God is doing in this hour is different. It's going to take power, it's going to take faith, it's going to take courage, and it's going to take strength. I love that it is Jesus! It says it right there in the Book of Hebrews: it's Him! Because of that, you can hold on to "the rejoicing of the hope." We need that hope. The enemy would come to steal all of your hope away.

Look To Jesus!

It tells us in Hebrews 12:2 to look to Jesus, who is the author and finisher of our faith. I like that. He doesn't just get us started. If we would look to Him, He's going to finish the work that He's begun. There is great hope in that: He can finish it. No matter who we are, no matter where we've come from, no matter the circumstances, the Perizzites, the Hittites, the Canaanites … no matter what is occupying our land. If Moses could do it, Jesus can do it better. The cry of my heart, and I believe each one of your hearts, is "Lord, let me go. Let my people go. Lord, let us be free from the bondage of those things that have held us back!"

We look to Jesus, and we think on Him. When I think about Jesus, I consider what we learn about Him in the Gospel of John. I love the way that John's Gospel is organized. It's so different than the others. I also love Matthew's, Mark's, and Luke's, but the Gospel of John is unique in that it revolves around seven "I Am" statements. Isn't it interesting that Jesus so fully knew who He was?

They are like a mission statement: This is who I am. I'm this, I'm this, I'm this … seven different truths. It's also beautiful to learn that each one of Jesus' "I Am" statements found in the Book of John correspond to a miracle He performed.

Like Jesus, we have to know who we are in order to do that which God has called us to do! Otherwise, we rely on happenstance. We hope to stumble into something. Have you ever felt the conviction of the Holy Spirit after missing a God-ordained moment? In retrospect, you feel, "Oh, I should have prayed for that person." When we walk around with a deep knowledge of who are in Christ, we are more intimately connected with the place God has called us to be! We won't miss those moments because we are more aware of who we are and what we are called to do.

We're not going to be effective in what He's called us to do unless we first understand who we are. Let's look at the example of Jesus, who truly knew who He was, even as a young boy.

I Must Be About My Father's Business

Luke 2:43-49 *When they had finished the days, as they returned, the Boy Jesus lingered behind in Jerusalem. And Joseph and His mother did not know it; but supposing Him to have been in the company, they went a day's journey, and sought Him among their relatives and acquaintances. So when they did not find Him, they returned to Jerusalem, seeking Him Now so it was that after three days they found Him in the temple, sitting in the midst of the teachers, both listening to them and asking them questions. And all who heard Him were astonished at His understanding and answers.*
So when they saw Him, they were amazed; and His mother said to Him, "Son, why have You done this to us? Look, Your father and I have sought You anxiously." And He said to them, "Why did you seek Me? Did you not know that I must be about My Father's business?"

This is an amazing account. Think about it. A 12-year-old is missing! Imagine you're traveling, and your 12-year-old decides to stay behind without informing you! Jesus' parents, Mary and Joseph, didn't notice right away that Jesus was missing. They were traveling with a big family group, so Mary and Joseph probably thought to themselves, "Jesus must be walking with his cousin, other relatives, or friends." Once they realized they could not find Him in their group, they returned to Jerusalem.

They were already one day's journey out from Jerusalem, and the journey back would take a day. In verse 46, it says that they didn't find him until after 3 days, which means they must have been searching around for him in Jerusalem (anxiously, I'm sure!) for another day! Finally, they find Jesus in a very unexpected place. They lived in a society that had distinct stratas. A 12-year-old boy would never be permitted to sit with the teachers in the temple. Jesus, though, knew who He was. He was sitting in the midst of the teachers, both listening to them and asking them questions. Who Jesus was compelled the teachers enough to keep Him in the room!

When we walk in the anointing that God has given us, when we understand who we really are, there is a favor that rests on us. Opportunities come along that you walk into because you know where you belong. It doesn't matter what people may say. Somebody may say to you, "You don't belong there," but you say, "Oh yes, I do. I do! I know who I am in God."

In our story, Jesus is asking the teachers questions and listening to their answers. The people there were astonished at His understanding and answers. When Mary scolded Jesus and asked why He had done this, Jesus said that they shouldn't be surprised. He had to be about the Father's business.

I believe that we are going to be asking the Lord, "Lord, what is the Father's business for me? What is the vision that You would have for me?" Just as Jesus knew who He was and what He was called to do, we will be able to bypass that which would prevent us from walking in all the Lord has called us to be and to do.

I believe today's question for each one of us is, "Who are you?" The answer is going to be different for each one of us. We cannot waste our time being someone other than ourselves. We can't do it!

You can't be like the person who is next to you; you can't try to be like the pastor. Can we admire people? Can we follow people, like Paul, who said, "Follow me as I follow Christ"? Sure, but that doesn't mean that we're supposed to be them.

We need to be ourselves! We need to be who we are! There's a power in your uniqueness, and the Lord wants to bring clarity out of the confusion of who you are really called to be.

You Are Unique!

This message of uniqueness has resonated in my spirit for decades. I've been a Christian for over 40 years. During that time, as prophets would come and prophesy over me, it would inevitably make my dear friend laugh: Almost every time a prophet would speak over me, they would use the word "unique." I hated it! I didn't want to be unique.

I wanted to look like everybody else; I wanted to fall in line with everybody else. She would be laughing, and I would say, "No, not again! Not this 'unique' thing!" Thank God that I've come to appreciate my uniqueness all these years later. I don't hate it any more - I embrace it!

Recently, I taught a New Testament survey class. It's a fascinating study on so many levels. The New Testament has 27 different books and many different authors. There's Matthew, there's Mark, there's Luke, there's John, there's Paul, there's Peter. You can think about who has written the different books. Then, you can study the different people that they talk about, whether it's Timothy, Barnabas, or Ananias. What I love about this now, that I didn't appreciate when I was younger, is that each author has a unique perspective.

Have you ever wondered why are there four gospels? Wouldn't it be enough to just have one? The Lord says, "No, I want you to see things from different perspectives." It's the same story, but it's different perspectives of it.

The same thing holds true with us today. We all have unique personalities. We look different, and we have different experiences. If you look at the people in the New Testament, some, like Dr. Luke, were well educated, while some were absolutely not. Some lacked the ability to chronicle details. Despite their differences, God called them according to their talents; according to their personality; according to their natural and spiritual giftedness.

Someone like Luke, who was obviously brilliant, gave the most detailed account of the gospels. Someone like Mark was interested in what Jesus did, so he wrote a gospel that focused on Jesus' miracles. When you look at someone like Paul, who was a Pharisee of the Pharisees, and you look at some of the things that he wrote, they were brilliant! Why? God created him that way. Some of the people of the New Testament were wealthy; some were poor.

Some were married and some were not. A look at Peter's life and personality shows that he was very emotional and impulsive. He was quick to fly off the handle, but quick to repent, too. Paul was an extremely focused person, whose words and actions suggested, "Don't get in my way because I've got a whole bunch of stuff to do." Barnabas was a very compassionate person, willing to mediate between people when problems arose. Luke, being the only Gentile who wrote anything in the New Testament, came from a whole different background. It's amazing to me that God would do that! Think about the Apostle John: he was like a poet and philosopher.

You read the Gospel of John, 1,2, 3 John, and the Book of Revelation, and it's pretty far out there! John was having visions and all sorts of things. You look at Agabus, a prophet in the Book of Acts, who didn't think it was enough to say, "Thus saith the Lord ..." He demonstrated it! He was dramatic and liked to act. At one point, Agabus told Paul what was going to happen to him by literally acting it out. Take a look at John the Baptist: he wore a bunch of weird clothes, ate really strange food, and sat out in the desert, shouting!

What's my point? I purposefully chose to highlight people from the New Testament, but the Old Testament is full of unique characters, too! Think of Ezekiel: lying on one side, then lying on the other side. It's all pretty strange! The Lord includes the quirks and personalities of these Biblical characters for us to learn something that we need to know.

He's asking us a question: Why do you think that now, in this generation, every Christian should fit a certain mold? Why? Why should we all be alike? In this hour, the Lord desires to bring forth His multi-faceted Body that recognizes and appreciates the differences.

I love to read biographies. One of my favorite books is Sister Aimee. When you look at the life of Aimee Semple McPherson, you realize she was … wild! Kathryn Kuhlman - wild! Smith Wigglesworth - wild! These people were so different from one another, and they were ridiculed in their day. Smith Wigglesworth wasn't well educated, and he had an abrupt way of saying things. You may have heard some of the stories about him. The Lord would use him and say This person is going to be healed, and he'd even hit them at times! Okay, that's weird. That's very unusual. You look at Kathryn Kuhlman, and she dressed in crazy outfits; it was part of her dramatic personality. I love it, because each one was unique; they had unusual traits, unusual personalities, and unusual style.

There is not supposed to be one, cookie-cutter type of Christian. The uniqueness of these leaders, pastors, prophets, and teachers ministers in a special way. The uniqueness of the New Testament authors powerfully ministers to us. Likewise, I believe our uniqueness also ministers to the Body. There is such a pressure to conform: It's not only in the world; sadly, it's in the Church, too. As the Holy Spirit opens our eyes to see it, I pray that He supernaturally anoints us with answers and sets us free from the trap the enemy has set for us.

Make It Personal

1. Have you ever felt like an outsider, even (or especially) at church? If so, have you attempted to change your God-given nature to "fit in?" What are some ways you can reclaim your true identity in Christ?

2. How would you compare your concepts/opinions of the Old Testament to the New Testament of the Bible? Have you had a preference for the teachings of the New Testament or found them more relevant/accessible? Why do you think God chose to speak to us through the stories and characters in the Old Testament? How might these reasons relate to Jesus' use of parables in the New Testament?

3. As Christians, how can we still find ourselves in bondage/slavery in Egypt? What deeper levels of freedom are you crying out for in your spirit today?

4. Are there people in your life whom you desire to be like? Where is the line between healthy admiration and wanting to be someone you are not?

5. Have you been able to relate to certain heroes of the faith more than others, based on their personality or unique background? Fisherman, doctor, tax collector? Peace-maker, fireball, highly dramatic? What about people you know or people you've read about? How has their uniqueness ministered to you?

CHAPTER 2

There Will Be A Form!

I believe we all are prone to have "Gunne Sax dresses" in our lives. It doesn't have to be clothes; it can be a way of speaking, or perhaps what priorities we have adopted. It can be anything that we take hold of that isn't authentic to us. It's the pressure of conformity. The Lord would have you know that you are a unique creation! You have an unique testimony, and you're meant to have a unique impact. If you divorce yourself from who God has made you to be, you cannot be all that the Lord would have you to be. There is a power and anointing that comes from walking in our unique identity.

The Book of Genesis says that God created everything uniquely. God says, "I want this uniqueness - whatever the species is - to replicate after its own kind." You have to be so clear on who and what you are in order to impart it into other people. That doesn't mean that we turn them into who we are. Rather, God gives us a certain portion, a certain anointing, a certain package to deliver. If we say, "Well, my package is no good. I need what that person has," we're never going to be able to do it. We don't want to waste time trying to be someone else because we can only impart what we ourselves possess.

The Greatness Of You!

James 1:8 states, "A double minded man is unstable in all his ways." When we are not clear on who we are, we can't do very much! When you consider the human body, it takes nine months to be formed. Isn't that fascinating?

With a dog, it takes two months - a 60-day gestation - and the dog pops out furry and almost ready to walk. If you've ever witnessed the birth of very large animals, they stand up almost immediately. With a human, it takes nine months in the womb and then about 18 years after that! It takes a year for most babies to begin walking, and it takes a long time to talk and learn all the components needed to communicate. Scientists say that the human brain isn't fully formed until it's close to 18-years-old. Not everything is fully wired yet. Why is that? It's because God is doing something highly detailed with His people. It's so creative! It's such a deep work that it takes time to form. It's important.

In the Old Testament, we find a series of people who all went through the same experience: barrenness. (Anytime we see something repeated over and over in the Scriptures, it's highlighting a truth for us to take hold of in our lives!) When I look at all the stories that come under the theme of The Miraculous Sons of Barrenness, I realize that there is wisdom to learn and apply to our own lives. Over and over, we see the great heroes of the Old Testament struggling to have children but later overcoming their barrenness with the birth of a child. That pattern is interesting to me.

Let's look at the birth of Isaac. His parents, Abraham and Sarah, struggled greatly to have children, despite every promise of God regarding their offspring. The same thing happened in the next generation with the birth of Jacob. His parents, Rebekah and Isaac, had to overcome barrenness. Likewise, in the story of the birth of Joseph, Rachel is filled with grief over her lack of children for many years.

The pattern repeated generation after generation after generation. How about Samuel the prophet? We discover his mother, Hannah, in 1 Samuel, tormented before Samuel was born with her inability to conceive. The same is true regarding the birth of Samson. He was a miraculous son of parents who struggled with barrenness.

24

John the Baptist's parents couldn't have children until he was conceived. Jesus' virgin conception is the ultimate miraculous birth, right? Jesus is a miraculous Son who comes forth! Why is it that this theme repeats over and over? It's because we are just like them!

It wasn't easy for you to get where you are. Each of our stories is miraculous. Whether or not you've grown up in a Christian home, it's amazing that you're reading this book right now and saying, "Yes!" to the Lord. "Lord, whatever You want to do." That's a miraculous birthing by the power of the Holy Spirit. Just like Samson, just like Samuel, just like Isaac, just like all of the miraculous sons, your life and your testimony is purposeful, and it's important. Yes, there might be some scars and some wounds that you've gotten along the way, but even so, you're here! That means that you've been born into the purpose of God. You're at the point where you say, "Lord, I want to fulfill what You've made me to be and to do." I love what Paul writes in Philippians 3:12: "Not that I have already attained, or am already perfected; but I press on, that I may lay hold of that for which Christ Jesus has also laid hold of me." God wants that to stir in our spirits! For the rest of our lives, let us say, "Lord, I want to be busy about the Father's business for my life. I want to be authentically me, fulfilling all that You've called me to be."

Every Part Of The Body Is Important

Let's take a look at a powerful passage of Scripture from 1 Corinthians 12:14-21.

1 Corinthians 12:14-15 *For in fact the body is not one member but many. If the foot should say, "Because I am not a hand, I am not of the body," is it therefore not of the body?*

A couple years ago, I broke two bones in my foot. Strangely, I broke my foot just as I was starting to heal from breaking two bones in my hand! I experienced a few months of difficulty and inability. I learned something interesting during that healing process though. I discovered that breaking a foot affects life much differently than breaking a hand. It became clear to me that we need every single part of the body to function! This scripture is saying that the foot can't be down on itself because it's not a hand. How weird would that be? It's equally wrong if we say, "Well, I'm not like this person over here at church, so therefore I'm not really part of the Body." No! That person is them, and I'm me.

1 Corinthians 12:16 *And if the ear should say, "Because I am not an eye, I am not of the body," is it therefore not of the body?*

I like what this illustrates to us. Imagine if someone with a prophetic ability to hear would say, "Well, I'm not much of a seer in the Body of Christ; I can only hear." Wouldn't it be sad if the person who hears the voice of the Lord would say, "Well, I'm really not that important."?

1 Corinthians 12:17-18 *If the whole body were an eye, where would be the hearing? If the whole were hearing, where would be the smelling? But now God has set the members, each one of them, in the body just as He pleased.*

You are who you are because it pleased God. He said, "I've got a plan and a purpose. I'm going to form you for nine months. I'm going to take My time. You're going to have these experiences . . ." and all the various ingredients that make you the unique creation that God intended.

1 Corinthians 12:19-21 *And if they were all one member, where would the body be? But now indeed there are many members, yet one body. And the eye cannot say to the hand, "I have no need of you"; nor again the head to the feet, "I have no need of you."*

God's plan for His Body is for there to be different individuals who stand together in unity. We must understand that we don't have to be the same to have unity; rather, we are stronger when we walk in unity with our differences.

I have a two-fold purpose in writing this book: first, for you to discover who you are; and second, for you to receive everyone else with their God-given identity and uniqueness.

There are issues with both of these aspects in the Body of Christ today. When we discover who we are and begin to move out in it, we shouldn't then lack the grace to receive other members of the Body. They are equally important! We must not have the attitude of, "I don't know where they're coming from!" when others don't see things the way we do. No, we need to recognize another's God-given purpose. They're doing and seeing things differently because we need them! That is what John 17 is all about. That's why Jesus so powerfully prays to the Father, "Lord, that they might be one even as we are one." Jesus is not suggesting that He would be the Father and the Holy Spirit would be the Son!

Each member of the Trinity has a distinct role! Jesus is proclaiming in this prayer that He, the Father, and the Holy Spirit are one in the great kingdom purpose. Our prayer needs to be, "Lord, may the Body of Christ be one in the great kingdom purpose." I believe this is God's heart's desire. I believe that the Lord desires to eliminate envy and jealousy.
He wants to begin to change our perspective as we become confident in who we are called to be. We are not going to be jealous of what others are called to be, but we are going to roll out the carpet for them and say, "Be you!" Can you feel that in your spirit? He wants to do this two-fold work in each one of us. Be you, and let others be themselves! Oh, what great power and impact the Church will have as we walk together in unity.

Each one of us, like Esther, has come to the kingdom for such a time as this. There are so many people to touch. I'm fascinated with the scripture that says to look up and look at the harvest - it's white and ready to go! Instead of saying to hurry up and get out there (though we need to do that!), it says, "Pray, therefore to the Lord of the harvest that He would send forth laborers into the field." (Matthew 9:38) To this end, we need to accept one another, because each individual holds a great key and purpose in the harvest.

1 Corinthians 12:4 *There are diversities of gifts, but the same Spirit.*

You and I are different, but we have the same Holy Spirit; we have the same ultimate Kingdom goal. We have the same One who is leading us into all things. Though each gifting and each member is diverse, the Holy Spirit remains the same.

1 Corinthians 12:11 *But one and the same Spirit works all these things, distributing to each one individually as He wills.*

We need to remember this. God gives each one of us different gifts according to His will. They are given according to His great Master Plan. We need to be content with that which God has given us. We also need to avoid being intimidated by what God has given us! Everything is given according to His plan.

He wants us to have it because there is something He wants us to do with it. We need to be content with what God has given other people and not be intimidated by it, but also not be envious of it. If God raises up the next Billy Graham, and he is sitting right next to us, we need to say, "I'm going to pray for you; I'm going to believe for this! You go! I want to see you do it." If God raises up the next great prophetic voice right next to us, we say, "Yes! Speak it! Let's pray for this!" Simultaneously, we need to walk in whatever He's called us to do.

In this hour, I believe the Lord is wanting to eliminate any reluctance to walk in that which He has created us to be. This reluctance or intimidation is like a Perizzite or a Canaanite - He wants to eliminate them from our lives. He wants us to be strong and of a good courage in order to knock out the enemy and take the land! He wants us to walk into this dimension and have our faces set for that which is ahead. May we be those who would say, "I know what I'm called to do!"

God Has A Blueprint!

One of our theme scriptures needs to be Jeremiah 1:5!

Jeremiah 1:5 *Before I formed you in the womb I knew you; Before you were born I sanctified you; I ordained you a prophet to the nations.*

In other words, God is saying, "I had the blueprints, and I knew exactly what I was doing." The circumstances of your birth don't matter. Even if your parents thought they didn't want you, God wanted you! He had the blueprint, and He said, "Now is the time to bring this person forth!" Jeremiah 1:5 says that we have been sanctified, which means set apart. I love that! God said, "Nina, I've set you apart, and I have ordained you!"

I deeply appreciate the part of Abraham and Sarah's story when they were struggling to conceive Isaac. We will take a closer look at their story soon, but the Scriptures make it clear that God had a set time for Isaac to be born. In a place of barrenness, God had appointed a time for the barrenness to end. When Isaac finally came forth, it says, "and at the set time Isaac was born." I also find it encouraging that God had already given him a name!

God has had something unique in mind for us from before we were born. The blueprints may look crazy, but He drew them up before time began. God has all the ingredients working together in His master recipe. He formed you with your destiny in mind. Therefore, there is no place for us to think, "Well, if only I was a seventh-generation preacher, then I might have a chance..." No! He gave you your parents, your background, your situation, the hard things that you've been through, the wounds that you've had to endure, as well as the obstacles that have been in your path. God allowed them. He may not have caused them, but He allowed them. Here's the reason: He is shaping you to fulfill your great destiny! You're not alive to fulfill my destiny. You are alive to fulfill your destiny.

In the Book of Genesis, we find another great example of God's blueprint in the story of Joseph. Joseph endures a long list of crazy, horrible things! It begins when he is betrayed by his own brothers. When we suffer hurts and abuses, we can think, "Well, I can never get over this, or this is why I'll never be able to accomplish everything God has called me to do." No! Joseph suffers his brothers' betrayal. Then, he is sentenced to slavery (right there, most of us would throw in the towel)! He is falsely accused and sent to prison. Then, through a miraculous event, orchestrated by God, Joseph is brought forth out of prison into the house of Pharaoh to fulfill the great destiny on his life. Through Joseph's wisdom and anointing, he is able to save the nations of the earth from famine. He also saves his brothers' lives and reconciles with them. I love what Joseph says to his brothers, who betrayed him. I have this scripture framed on the wall of my office. It is Genesis 50:20.

Genesis 50:20 *But as for you, you meant evil against me; but God meant it for good, in order to bring it about as it is this day, to save many people alive.*

We can imagine that Joseph's brothers were thinking, "We thought Joseph was dead after we betrayed him, but he's alive! Now, we're begging him for food. He's going to kill us!" Instead, Joseph says, "The things that you meant for evil, God meant for good. The brothers had planned to kill Joseph those many years earlier. His life was spared when one of his brothers suggested selling him into slavery instead of murdering him. That's a pretty enormous offense for Joseph to forgive. Joseph not only got over it, though; he also saved his brothers' lives. When we know that the Lord is orchestrating our lives, we can walk in forgiveness and know that even the difficult things are serving God's purposes for us! The difficulties in our lives are our qualifying course to fully understand that God is able. He's all-powerful. God is omniscient: He knows everything. He knows the ingredients that are needed for the master recipe He is preparing.

The Conformity Of Church Culture

I sometimes laugh at how much conformity I see in the Body of Christ! Perhaps because I was an "outsider" when I got saved, I see it so clearly now. When I first came into the Church, I was very sensitive to the church culture.

It felt like its own nation that had customs: Here's how we dress; here's how we talk; here's how we speak in "Christianese." Now, being a lot older and somewhat wiser, I can ask, "Why wouldn't the Creator be creative?" He created an infinite number of stars. We don't even know where they all are! Why did He do this? He likes variety; He likes differences. How about the animals that humans still haven't discovered? How about the fish that nobody has seen yet? As soon as something new is discovered, we think, "Oh my goodness, that's incredible!" Well, that's what He's doing with us. He loves that we're unique and different from one another. We don't have to be at odds with what God intended us to be. We have freedom to be different.

There is often a big gap between where we stand today and the life/identity God shaped for us before our birth. It can be an interference by the enemy. We must remember that God is the God of restoration! He is here to heal us and to restore us. We ask, "Who are we, and have we lost our true identity?" There are things that distort our identity. There are things that prevent us from realizing our destiny. There are situations and events in life from which we can develop fear, confusion, and a lack of confidence. I like what Luke 19:10 tells us.

Luke 19:10 *For the Son of Man has come to seek and to save that which was lost.*

Is this referring to our salvation? Absolutely. That's the first, foundational, and primary element, but Jesus has also come to restore all that He has for us.

We already read Jeremiah 1:5, which talks about being formed in the womb. Sadly, we often lose our proper form.

Conformed Or Transformed?

Romans 12:1-2 *I beseech you therefore, brethren, by the mercies of God, that you present your bodies a living sacrifice, holy, acceptable to God, which is your reasonable service. And do not be conformed to this world, but be transformed by the renewing of your mind, that you may prove what is that good and acceptable and perfect will of God.*

The word "beseech" means to beg. In this letter to believers, Paul is begging us to do something. He is saying that it involves presenting our whole self, our whole life. Paul is asking believers to have their minds renewed!

God wants to renew our minds because our greatest issues stem from what is going on inside our minds. Carefully notice the wording in this passage. Paul writes to "not to be conformed...but be transformed." Look at those two words. They both involve a form.

There is always going to be a form. It may not be the form God intended for us though. We can be either conformed or transformed. When choose to conform, I believe there are several subcategories. 1. We can be unformed, where we are in a constant state of waiting to become something. Instead of allowing God to form us, we are in a sort of holding pattern. 2. We can be, what I call, performed. In this state, our primary motivation is for people to like and approve of us. To this end, we will perform to earn the approval of man. 3. We can also be deformed. When our lives veer far away from where God wants us to be, we can begin to resemble something He never intended.

Some people spend their whole lives unformed. They never make a decision; they never take a risk. They might think, "Well, I don't want to possibly make a mistake." The Lord is so gracious! Think of the story of Peter, as he sees Jesus walking on the water. Of course, Peter had never seen anybody do this before! Peter wants to join Jesus and says, "Jesus, bid me to come." Jesus beckons him, and it starts out okay. Then, Peter gets concerned and thinks, "This is defying gravity!" Peter begins to sink, but the Lord doesn't rebuke him. There are times when we need to take a step. Even if it doesn't work out completely, there's something important about stepping out: It takes faith. I believe that the Lord honors it, and He helps us to grow from it. We can't live in a state of perpetual "safety" from failure.

That's what we learn from the parable about burying our talents. The Lord wants us to take the gifts He has given us and multiply them. There is risk involved, but we step out, trusting the Lord will guide us. If we sink, He will lift us up; and, in the process, we will have grown in our faith and in our giftings. I believe that one of the great keys of stepping out in faith is staying humble, so that we can allow correction to come. If we go a little too far in our faith, someone might come along and say, "I think you started well, but next time maybe you could change this..." The correction is good, because that's where we learn.

I love the scripture in Philippians where it says, "I press towards the mark of the high call." There's some pressing that goes on, and, in the press, we're wrong sometimes. That's okay! It takes courage to correct our course, but this is what it takes if we don't want to be unformed.

Some people spend their whole life trying to perform for others. They perform for their mom, for their dad, for the people around them. These are the people who are always looking for approval. What would have happened if Moses had said, "I can't do anything! I don't have the stamp of approval from Pharoah. I don't even have consensus amongst the people of Israel." The Israelites were coming to Moses saying, "Who in the world do you think you are? Why are you taking on all of this power?" We need to be so careful to obey God by doing the things He has asked us to do.

Yes, there is the context of proper government, proper church-life, and proper authority in our lives. However, if we're always trying to take a vote and make sure everyone is on board, we can fall into a performance trap. "Does everybody think that I should do it?" There are going to be times when God will say in the Spirit, "Who will go for Me?" He's looking for a people who would say, "Here am I, Lord, send me." Others may say, "You are crazy! I don't see God in this.

I would never go. This isn't right." I can't tell you how many times people have told me that women shouldn't preach. What should I do with that? I believe the Scriptures say I should. I believe the Lord has called me to preach. My pastor believes in my call and supports me. My husband believes I'm called to it and supports me. With that, I can listen when others reject the idea of women preaching but still turn around and know that this is the call of God on my life. We need to be those who are not just performing to get accolades.

I've read articles about how social media is designed to subconsciously encourage people to seek approval from other people. It causes users to compulsively check to see if others saw and "liked" what they wrote or posted. We must not be governed by others' opinions of us! We want our motivation to be in doing the Father's business.

Some people have been so damaged that they become deformed. They may allow themselves to become deformed because they are embittered by what has come their way in life. It's interesting that Hebrews 12:15 says "a bitter root grows up to cause trouble and defile many."

What would have happened if Joseph had not forgiven his brothers? If he had sought revenge for the wrongs he suffered, he would have missed his entire destiny. Nations would have suffered famine if Joseph had chosen bitterness over forgiveness.

2 Timothy 3:5 *Having a form of godliness but denying its power. And from such people turn away!*

We can also take on a form that's just religious. The Bible says that the Pharisees loved to be heard praying. They enjoyed being acknowledged for their offerings. There were careful to clothe themselves in all of the religious garments. They vied for the best seat in the house. The heart of the Pharisees asked, "Did everyone see what I just did? Aren't I awesome?" That is a deformity as well. We don't want to just have a form of godliness, but we want the power behind it!

If you are called to be someone like John the Baptist, your head may be cut off, like his was! It's not all glory and riches! We need to ask, "Will I have the courage to do what God has called me to?" This is the question Esther had to answer. She realized that doing what God called her to do could mean getting killed. Mordecai, a type of the Holy Spirit, speaks into her life and says, "You can make the decision that you want." God gives us choices. You don't have to be who God has called you to be! Mordecai continues by saying, "If you don't, God will surely use another."

It's such a great privilege to take risks, to move in the flow of the Holy Spirit, and to be willing to do that which the Lord desires of you. We can't accomplish all that the Lord has called us to do as a lone wolf. That is part of the beauty of a local church. We need to answer to people; we need to have others to speak into our lives.

Freedom To Be You

As God is saying, "Who are you? Who have I called you to be?", I believe He is also asking, "What form are you going to take?" There's a freedom coming!

Philippians 3:12-14 *Not that I have already attained, or am already perfected; but I press on, that I may lay hold of that for which Christ Jesus has also laid hold of me. Brethren, I do not count myself to have apprehended; but one thing I do, forgetting those things which are behind and reaching forward to those things which are ahead, I press toward the goal for the prize of the upward call of God in Christ Jesus.*

Paul writes that he is going to forget those things that are behind and reach forward to those things which are ahead! That's exactly what God wants us to do! His mercies are new every morning. Whatever went on up until now doesn't matter, because we have a new start right now! Right now, God is saying, "Are you going to press forward? Will you allow Me to change you and give you a courage that will impact others for eternity?"

Look at the story of Stephen in Acts 6-7. It's an incredible story, isn't it? Stephen is serving lunches to the old ladies, and he has such a powerful anointing on his life that he is impacting people. No matter how you're serving, the anointing can be there; the anointing in the most mundane tasks can be powerful! Stephen is serving lunches, and apparently, what he's saying is so powerful that he is arrested.

That's a pretty amazing lunch server! The Jewish leaders are ready to kill him, and he begins to preach a sermon. This appeals to me! Stephen preaches a sermon that is so revelatory that it changes the nations! We discover later in the scriptures that Saul, who became Paul the Apostle, was standing right there at Stephen's stoning.

Stephen's message deeply affected Paul's life, and Paul went on to impact the nations of the earth by the power of the Holy Spirit. As Stephen was preaching and being stoned, there were people in the crowd who literally put their fingers in their ears. The words that he spoke with the anointing of the Holy Spirit convicted their hearts in such a way that they could not bear it!

To some, the Word of God was unto salvation, and to others, it produced the same effect Jesus' words had on the religious leaders: "We have to kill this person!" Thank God that the fingers-in-ears crowd didn't discourage Stephen to the point that he would not speak.

Since we all know we're going to die at some point, I like the idea of going with a big bang! Without dying prematurely, I want to come to the end of my life and say, like Paul, "I've finished my race. I've completed that which I was called to do." Paul also says, "I'm ready to be offered." I love the idea of completely accomplishing what God has for me and standing before Jesus to hear Him say, "Well done! You did it! You did what I specifically formed you to do: what I called you to do, gifted you to do, and gave you the circumstances to do."

I believe we're in a prophetic moment that asks us to stop trying to be something we're not. Jesus knew that He was the Lamb slain from the foundation of the earth. That's why, at 12-years-old, He could say, "Mom and Dad, didn't you know? I had to be about the Father's business."

Identity Theft!

Don't you find it interesting that one of the biggest concerns in modern life is identity theft? There are whole companies that work to make sure that your social security number and credit card numbers aren't stolen. These companies know right away if someone else is using your credit card.

A couple years ago, when my mom passed away, our lawyer instructed me to immediately send out notices to the credit agencies regarding her death. Otherwise, people could steal her identity by looking at the obituaries. If you've ever known someone who has had their identity stolen, it is a mess! You have to prove who you are, and it's a difficult process.

We need to ask ourselves, "Have I kept track of my identity, of who I am in Christ? Has the enemy captured my sense of self? Has my identity been taken hostage by the enemy?" The demonic pressure to conform may be greater in this generation than it has ever been. Even though we think that everyone is "doing their thing," the pressure of comparing oneself to others is unprecedented. We receive countless messages about who we should be. They come from the media, our music, and even political correctness. This is all part of conformity. If we dare to come against what the politically-correct thought is, we are completely shunned. Boycotts happen regularly in response to what society doesn't accept. There is a tremendous force. We must rise up with courage to be all that the Lord intends for us to be.

What about unrealistic body images? They can be giant stumbling blocks that derail people's lives. We can think, "I'm too fat. I'm too skinny. I'm too short. I'm too tall. I don't look pretty." What lies from the devil! Even the people we look at in magazines don't actually look like that. The images have all been processed and airbrushed. We're trying to conform to an ideal that doesn't even exist. I believe there has never been more confusion over our identity.

How about credit card debt? I believe it can come from a lack of knowing who we really are. We're busy spending money we don't have in order to look like we've achieved a lifestyle someone else is purporting we should have! "You've GOT to have those shoes.

You've GOT to have this purse. You've got to have your hair looking this way." Why?! If you don't have the money, then, no, it's not what you need. Who you truly are - not the person the identity thief wants you to be - is so powerful.

You Can Be Different!

You are free to be different! You don't have to be like someone else. You can break the conformity of this world. You can have the courage to do that for your own life and stand up for others who are being "bullied." Let's be believers who will not receive gossip about another person. Let's not stand by while people are cutting someone else down, "I didn't like what they said. I don't like the way they look." No. Let us be ones who stand up and say, "No! That person is awesome! God is calling them forth!" If something is wrong, then let's pray for them. Let's come alongside them! God is raising us up to not be conformed to the world.

Consider Samson. Many people only remember Samson's sin, but there's so much more to the story! (Remember: these Old Testament stories are historical events that are also for our learning and admonition.) Samson was all about his hair. When we look at the story of Samson in the Book of Judges, we discover that his hair represented his uniqueness. It was the source of his power, and God instructed him to never cut his hair. The enemy couldn't stand him because he was called to be a deliverer for Israel. He was raised up in his generation to be a judge in Israel. He had great victories.

No one was stronger than Samson. The Philistines, Israel's enemy, thought, "Hmm, we have to knock him down a notch." Likewise, the enemy says of each one of us, "I've got to knock her down. I've got to knock him down. I'll try to destroy the thing that God has uniquely made them to be."

The enemy schemes and plots behind the scenes and sends in a beautiful lady. He does this knowing that Samson has a weakness for the ladies. Delilah's entire role is to find an answer to, "Samson, what makes you so strong?" At first, Samson is on to the game, and he won't tell her.

She comes daily, pressing him to give her an answer. Notice that Samson's responses get progressively closer and closer to the truth. "Well, it's the way my hair is braided." Each time Samson replies, Delilah tells the Philistines, and they come in to destroy him. Unbelievably, Samson doesn't perceive, "Oh, they're out to get me, and Delilah is in on it." Delilah even has the gall to say, "Why didn't you tell me the truth?" Delilah whines to Samson, "Oh, come on, Samson! You have to tell me what it is!" Samson finally says, "It's my hair." His hair is then cut by her, the enemy comes in, and Samson has no strength to fight them. The Philistines take him as a captive. They poke his eyes out and put him in bondage.

The enemy is constantly trying to pull that number on us, too! When we are not who we are supposed to be, we lose our vision. We can end up being in bondage, captive to the enemy. That's why the cry of the Holy Spirit is, "Let My people go!"

I love the end of Samson's story. When the revelation of Samson's story hit me, I was studying Hebrews 11, which is all about the heroes of the faith. I noticed that Samson made the list of heroes, and I thought, "Wow, God! You see him as a hero?" I began to study Samson's story in detail, and I believe the reason why he is considered a hero is not because of his great victories at the beginning.

Rather, it's because of his great victory at the end of his life. While he's in prison, chained, and tied to a pole, Samson begins to have a revelation. His hair begins to grow again. He rises up one final time and tears down two pillars. In that final act, he kills more Philistines than he ever had in his life.

We can rise up, no matter what's gone on before, no matter how our hair has been cut, no matter how our identity has been stolen, no matter who we have been with that we should not have been with, no matter what we have done that we should not have done!

Today is the day to say, "Lord, let my hair grow again! I want to be exactly who you've called me to be so that I can do that which You've called me to do." I believe that the Lord would ask each of us, "Who are your Delilahs?" Who or what has been robbing you?

As you meditate on this, and as you read the next chapters, I pray that the Lord will give you an awareness of what these things are. What has the enemy put into your life that is robbing you of who really are? What is it that has caused a distortion to come?

Make It Personal

1. Have you ever felt that you or your giftings are less important than someone else or their giftings? Has envy ever reared its head inside of you? How have you dealt with those feelings of jealousy, inferiority, or intimidation?

2. On the other end of the spectrum, have you ever felt that you or your giftings are more important than those around you? If so, how have you dealt with those feelings of superiority and self-importance?

3. Jesus' prayer to the Father was, "Lord, that they might be one even as we are one." Can you imagine some specific ways in your life and in your church that Jesus' desire for unity could be fulfilled?

4. We long to be transformed and not conformed. Do you relate to any of the subcategories of conformity we explored? Have you found yourself deformed, unformed, or performed? Have you had a form of godliness, denying its power?

CHAPTER 3

Are You The Sibling Or The Spouse?

I believe that fear is one of the greatest identity robbers that we encounter. Let's look at three separate accounts in the Book of Genesis that deal with fear and result in someone losing sight of their true identity.

1 John 4:18 *There is no fear in love; but perfect love casts out fear, because fear involves torment. But he who fears has not been made perfect in love.*

God's plan for us is to live without fear. I believe that the Lord will reveal what we are afraid of to each of us individually. My prayer is that you will discover that fear is often at the root of why we are not able to be everything the Lord has intended.

Three Similar Stories

Remember: when we see a pattern repeated in Scripture, we know that the Lord is highlighting a truth that He wants us to comprehend clearly. We saw this with the miraculous sons of barrenness. This is certainly the case with the three narratives we will look at in this chapter. I like to call these stories in Genesis, "Are You the Sibling or Are You the Spouse?" These three stories are nearly identical. Two of them involve Abraham and Sarah, and one involves Isaac and Rebekah. They happen in different places and at different times in Abraham and Sarah's life.

In fact, Abraham and Sarah's two stories happen more than 20 years apart.

Let's think about the Book of Genesis. It is like the "Who's Who" of stories. How does a story get included? Creation is a pretty big story. Adam and Eve and their fall: that's critical to include. The Tower of Babel is phenomenal. How about Noah? Humanity's salvation on a boat sounds a lot like Jesus. Enoch walked with God and was not - let's include that! Cain and Abel: important lesson to learn there. The story of Abraham, Isaac, and Jacob: they're the patriarchs of Israel. Joseph's story gets included for sure. To me, it is amazing that God constructs the Book of Genesis and says, "I'm going to have to tell the same story three times." Why is that? The point of the story is so important! It would be as if Noah has an ark, and later, Joe has an ark, and now, let's have Mary with an ark... Would that strike you as strange? Isn't it enough to tell a story once? Interestingly, the story that occurs three times in the Book of Genesis is about identity theft. The stealing away of who we are is so critical to guard against that the Lord says, "The Book Genesis only has so much room, but I'm going to take a significant portion of it telling this story three times."

An Unfortunate Deception

In each of these three stories, a married couple decides to deny that they are husband and wife and instead claim that they are brother and sister. Why did they do it? We discover in these scriptures that they did it out of fear.

Let's begin by looking at Genesis 12:10-20.

Genesis 12:10-13 *Now there was a famine in the land, and Abram went down to Egypt to dwell there, for the famine was severe in the land. And it came to pass, when he was close to entering Egypt, that he said to Sarai his wife,*
"Indeed I know that you are a woman of beautiful countenance. "Therefore it will happen, when the Egyptians see you, that they will say, 'This is his wife'; and they will kill me, but they will let you live. Please say you are my sister, that it may be well with me for your sake, and that I may live because of you."

We have to recognize that hard times sometimes bring out fear in us. No doubt this is why the Lord spoke to Joshua and told him to be strong and courageous. Joshua was called to take land that had never been taken before. He was going into unfamiliar territory. Before Joshua, this was true for Abram and Sarai as well.

Previous to these verses in Genesis 12:10-15 is the call that came to Abram and Sarai. This barren couple is told that they are going to form a nation and that all the nations of the earth are going to be blessed. They are going to have children, or at least one child, who will have more children. Abram and Sarai are barren and quite elderly already! The scenario seems ridiculous. Have you ever felt that about the call of God on your life? If you know the call of God on your life, you might say, "There is no way! How could God ever say that? Everything in my life defies that expectation." Even at this point in the story, Abram and Sarai are already walking in a miracle. Sarai is older than 65, and Abram is so worried about her amazing beauty that he thinks, "They're going to kill me because you're that beautiful." They arrive on the scene: barren and fearful. They feel like the possibility of the birth of a child is so remote. Out of self-protection, Abram thinks, "I won't reveal who we really are." We must be careful to avoid an attitude that says, "This God-ordained destiny isn't going to happen anyway, so let me just try to figure out my life in a different way."

Genesis 12:14-15a *So it was, when Abram came into Egypt, that the Egyptians saw the woman, that she was very beautiful. The princes of Pharaoh also saw her and commended her to Pharaoh.*

The Egyptians say, "Wow! She is a knock-out!" They go and tell Pharaoh, "Wow, we've seen the new lady in town, and she is really something."

Genesis 12:15b-16 *And the woman was taken to Pharaoh's house. He treated Abram well for her sake. He had sheep, oxen, male donkeys, male and female servants, female donkeys, and camels.*

Abram's life is going really well right now! In fact, Sarai's life is going well, too! Sarai is in Pharaoh's house; Abram is getting rich. This is all pretty awesome, right? Let's see what happens next...

Abram, What Have You Done To Me?

Genesis 12:17-20 *But the Lord plagued Pharaoh and his house with great plagues because of Sarai, Abram's wife. And Pharaoh called Abram and said, "What is this you have done to me? Why did you not tell me that she was your wife? "Why did you say, 'She is my sister'? I might have taken her as my wife. Now therefore, here is your wife; take her and go your way." So Pharaoh commanded his men concerning him; and they sent him away, with his wife and all that he had.*

Responding to the famine, Abram and Sarai go down to Egypt. Out of fear, they say, "Let's not be who we're supposed to be; let's pose as something else."

I believe that we often act in the same way. We look at our lives and say, "If I am who I really know myself to be, it's going to cause trouble. People aren't going to like it; it might create all sorts of difficulties..." I experienced this early on in my Christian walk. Raised in a Jewish family, you can imagine that becoming a Christian wasn't on the list of things my Jewish parents would be proud of or want for me.

I had to make a decision about how I was going to proceed. Of course, I wasn't going to purposefully be rude to my family, but I had to be who I was. I had to be willing to suffer the potential consequences of this choice.

Here are Abram and Sarai, denying they are husband and wife, living as brother and sister. Let's stop and ponder this. It's the very rejection of their true identity that would prevent the promised child from coming forth. With this denial of their marriage relationship, they are not even going to be living in the same place. Can you imagine that we also make decisions to deny our God-given identity and, in that very act, sabotage God's promises regarding our destiny?

When we deny who we really are, it sabotages our ability to bring forth what God wants. To me, the strangest part of the story is when Pharaoh takes Sarai. Abram and Sarai prospered, but Pharaoh's house is plagued, and Pharaoh recognizes this. Pharaoh is a type of the world, and he says, "Why weren't you who you were supposed to be? Why didn't you tell me she was your wife?" Abram tells him, "Well, I feared that they would kill me." Why is that? Think about it! When we aren't who we are supposed to be, our life might still prosper. I think we will still go to heaven. We won't have the fullness of what we could have on this earth, but we might be rich and have all sorts of things go our way. What's remarkable is that the world is cursed. The world is plagued. We have to ask ourselves, "Who is suffering because I'm not who I'm supposed to be?"

Where The Fear Came From

Why were they so afraid? When we look at Abram and Sarai's story, it's typical of what can happen in our lives as well. There were several factors at this stage of their lives that made them afraid.

Genesis 11:28 *And Haran died before his father Terah in his native land, in Ur of the Chaldeans.*

Haran, Abram's brother, died. We know it was an untimely death because their father, Terah, hadn't died yet. It's tragic to have a sibling die. In addition, Abram's brother died in the place that they had come from: Ur. "Haran" means mountaineer, so keep that in mind. Secondly, Abram and Sarai are given this promise: "You're going to be the father of this nation." Instead of having children, they are barren. Not only that, but Abram's name means "High Father." He has a prophetic destiny, but it's not working out in his life. Have you ever had a prophetic word that doesn't look like it's coming to pass?

Genesis 11:31 *And Terah took his son Abram and his grandson Lot, the son of Haran, and his daughter-in-law Sarai, his son Abram's wife, and they went out with them from Ur of the Chaldeans to go to the land of Canaan; and they came to Haran and dwelt there.*

In this verse, we see that Terah takes Abram, Lot, and Sarai from Ur to a place called Haran. How unusual! Terah took them to a place that has the same name as his Abram's deceased brother. Terah, Abram's father, died there. Abram has Lot with him. Lot's name means veil or blindfold. They have arrived at a place called Haran. Haran means mountaineer, so it speaks of knowing how to get up to the high places. However, there is a problem here. The brother whose name means mountaineer, isn't in the place called mountaineer. Abram may feel unequipped or inadequate to do the mountaineering that would have come naturally to Haran, his brother. Sometimes, a fear develops in us because we feel like someone else should be doing this. Isn't someone else more qualified than me to do this? Who am I to do this? Oh, that Haran wouldn't have died because we are now in the place called Haran!

God brings us into places where we are completely out of our element! It's like Peter walking on the water. Why should he be able to do it? It's because God called him to and said, "Come! I'll bid you to come." The Lord is bidding us to come into certain places. We may have fear that says, "Oh, now that He's called me, shouldn't there be someone else? Maybe the pastor should be doing it. Maybe someone like the Apostle Paul should be doing it. Certainly, it can't be me! If only they knew all of the issues, I wouldn't be the one to do this."

Genesis 12:1 *Now the LORD had said to Abram: "Get out of your country, From your family And from your father's house, To a land that I will show you."*

To paraphrase, this verse says, "Get out of your country, Abram. Get out or away from your kindred. Get out from your father's house, and I will make of you a great nation." Sometimes, when we are entirely out of our element and feel like we have been separated, it is then that the Lord can begin to move in a greater dimension in our lives. This happened to me in my own salvation experience. Why didn't I get saved earlier? It was probably because I was around everything that was familiar to me. In leaving that place of comfort and familiarity, I found myself somewhere that I knew no one, which enabled me to listen to and consider the Gospel message.

We need to realize that God does this after we are saved as well! He puts us into uncomfortable situations. I look at certain stories in the Scriptures, and I think, "Wow, they really had courage!" Think of the woman at the well in John 4. Jesus just revealed that He knew her sins, in having all these so-called "husbands" in her life. In the encounter, she realizes who He is. That's how it is in our walk with Christ! It's not about our qualifications; it's about God's qualifications. It's about encountering the Lord.

It says in John 4 that she becomes the first evangelist. She goes into the city and tells "everyone." Amazingly, everyone listens to her. Why? It's because she was being who she was called to be. Despite the shady past, she realizes, "I encountered Jesus, and, let me tell you, you've got to come and see the Man who told me everything." It's powerful!

Abram and Sarai are taken out of their comfort zones. They are given a call, but they are barren. How can that call possibly be true?

Genesis 12:9 *So Abram journeyed, going on still toward the South.*

"So Abram journeyed..." Let's not pass by that without taking note! Why do we develop fear? Sometimes, we question in our spirit, "How are we going to get there?" or "When are we going to get there?!"

Think about the story of Joseph. For thirteen years, he lived in a place of betrayal by his own brothers, followed by slavery and then prison. He had an amazing, prophetic dream going into it: "I see everybody bowing down," and he has his colorful coat of favor... Then, 13 years! Joseph was so sure of his destiny, but the dream was sorely tested in the subsequent 13 years. God causes us to come into situations where there are delays, but the Lord has a purpose in it.

As we continue on in Genesis 12, we read about why Abram and Sarai denied their true identity and relationship. It was because there was a famine. When things get dry, or when things get sparse, we begin to say, "Well, this dream or destiny is taking too long. I don't see any possible way that this is going to come together. I'm just going to give up...this looks like it's a waste of time."

The Same Thing Happens Again!

An astounding aspect of this story of denial is that Abram and Sarai don't learn their lesson the first time. Jumping ahead to Genesis 20, the very same circumstance happens a second time: 24 years later! Can you imagine a total repeat of this disastrous scenario? God needs to work this identity crisis completely out of our system. We will keep revisiting the same circumstances until we authentically become who we are supposed to be. The Lord desires that we would be who we are called to be and not deny our unique identity. When we aren't who we are supposed to be, we put ourselves into a situation where God won't bring forth what He desires.

Renamed now as Abraham and Sarah, we find the second story of them denying who they were in

Genesis 20:1-2: *And Abraham journeyed from there to the South, and dwelt between Kadesh and Shur, and stayed in Gerar. Now Abraham said of Sarah his wife, "She is my sister." And Abimelech king of Gerar sent and took Sarah.*

The great miracle of Sarah bringing forth a son is still at work. The call still remains. Twenty-four years have passed, and she is now 89-years-old. Sarah is still so beautiful, the king says, "She'll be mine."

In the very next verse, we read, *"But God came to Abimelech in a dream by night."* Do you see how this is the same story as Genesis 12?! In Genesis 12, God came to Pharaoh, and Pharaoh's house was plagued. Then, Pharaoh goes to Abram and Sarai, and he says, "What in the world are you doing to me?" The same thing happens here!

Genesis 20:3-5 *But God came to Abimelech in a dream by night, and said to him, "Indeed you are a dead man because of the woman whom you have taken, for she is a man's wife." But Abimelech had not come near her; and he said, "Lord, will You slay a righteous nation also? Did he not say to me, 'She is my sister'? And she, even she herself said, 'He is my brother.' In the integrity of my heart and innocence of my hands I have done this."*

Who You Are Impacts Others

What if the world is in the state that it's in because we aren't who we're supposed be? That should be a profound question for every single Christian to consider.

Genesis 20:6-7 *And God said to him in a dream, "Yes, I know that you did this in the integrity of your heart. For I also withheld you from sinning against Me; therefore I did not let you touch her. Now therefore, restore the man's wife; for he is a prophet, and he will pray for you and you shall live. But if you do not restore her, know that you shall surely die, you and all who are yours."*

If Abraham and Sarah aren't able to be who they're really supposed to be, Abimelech is going to die!

Genesis 20:8 *So Abimelech rose early in the morning, called all his servants, and told all these things in their hearing; and the men were very much afraid. And Abimelech called Abraham and said to him, "What have you done to us? How have I offended you, that you have brought on me and on my kingdom a great sin? You have done deeds to me that ought not to be done." Then Abimelech said to Abraham, "What did you have in view, that you have done this thing?"*
And Abraham said, "Because I thought, surely the fear of God is not in this place; and they will kill me on account of my wife. But indeed she is truly my sister. She is the daughter of my father, but not the daughter of my mother; and she became my wife.

And it came to pass, when God caused me to wander from my father's house, that I said to her, 'This is your kindness that you should do for me: in every place, wherever we go, say of me, "He is my brother." ' " Then Abimelech took sheep, oxen, and male and female servants, and gave them to Abraham; and he restored Sarah his wife to him. And Abimelech said, "See, my land is before you; dwell where it pleases you." Then to Sarah he said, "Behold, I have given your brother a thousand pieces of silver; indeed this vindicates you before all who are with you and before everybody." Thus she was rebuked. So Abraham prayed to God; and God healed Abimelech, his wife, and his female servants. Then they bore children; for the Lord had closed up all the wombs of the house of Abimelech because of Sarah, Abraham's wife.

The Difficulty Of Delay

As we look at this passage in Genesis 20, we see that 24 years had passed since they first learned the lesson about not denying who they really were. What's this about? It's all about delay! Delay can come and take its toll on our true identity. We can give up on what God has called us to do. There are two key Scriptures to remember during seasons of delay:

Galatians 6:9 *And let us not grow weary while doing good, for in due season we shall reap if we do not lose heart.*

Hebrews 6:12 *That you do not become sluggish, but imitate those who through faith and patience inherit the promises.*

This lesson happened twice because every single one of us are affected by seasons of delay. You have either already experienced the trial of delay, or, if you haven't yet experienced it, you inevitably will. Make a note it in your mind and heart today: there will come seasons of delay.

The Lord would say, "Don't give up in the seasons of delay!" The Lord desires for you to stand fast and be who God has called you to be even when it seems unfruitful. It is in the seasons of delay that our faith can be tried greatly, but it is strengthened as we see the promises of God come to pass. May we be those who would couple our faith with patience.

In Genesis 20, God is speaking to the king, the world leader, and says, "You're going to be a dead man." When we, as believes, are not who we are, people don't come into the Kingdom, and they surely are but a "dead man." We need to be those who look up and see the harvest. May we say, "Lord, send me as a laborer, and Lord, send other laborers." If we don't go forth as laborers, then the harvest isn't brought in, and they are but dead men.

Birthing An Ishmael

Previously, we saw some initial reasons as to why fear had crept in Abram and Sarai's lives. Now, 24 years later, new reasons for fear have come into their lives. What happened in the last two decades? We don't have time to look at it in detail, but you are probably familiar with these stories. Because of delay, Abram and Sarai hatch a plan for a son to come forth... just not by Sarai. They bring in Hagar, Sarai's servant, and, of course, she gets pregnant right away. Why is that? It's because when you're operating outside of your real identity and purposes, the enemy is more than happy to comply and make it look like you're fruitful. That "fruit," however, is an Ishmael and not an Isaac.

Ishmael is born. He creates a lot of trouble, and later on becomes an even bigger dilemma. You might imagine that a mistake like this might make all of God's promises null and void. Instead, we see that God changes Abram's name! "Abram" meant high father, which already spoke of his prophetic destiny.

Now, God changes his name to "Abraham," which means father of a multitude. Keep in mind that, at this part of the story, Abraham is 99-years-old. God allows us to come to impossible-looking places. God is saying, "Will there be a people who say, 'Even though it looks impossible, it's not by might, it's not by power, but it's by His Spirit, says the Lord.'?" God is looking for a people who are willing and able to believe He will to accomplish all He has declared.

There Is A Price To Pay

I love the story we read in Jeremiah 32. It takes place on the brink of Judah's captivity in Babylon. Jeremiah, the great prophet for the hour, is speaking the word of the Lord. In fact, Jeremiah prophesies the entire event of the captivity. Meanwhile, all sorts of false prophets speak forth false prophecies that sound good to the people and tell them what they want to hear.

All along, Jeremiah has been saying, "Repent, and if you are not repentant, you're going into Babylon." The king hates it so much that Jeremiah is arrested and put into prison. Now, sure enough, they are all going to be taken down into Babylon.

What a place for Jeremiah to be! Do you ever feel like you're in prison and that no one else is seeing what you're seeing? Have you ever been opposed by people who wear a form of godliness and say something contrary to what you feel God is speaking?

The story continues in Jeremiah 32, and God says, "Here's what's going to happen, Jeremiah. I'm going to send your uncle, Hanamiel, to you. He's going to offer you some land." That's a type to us of the promised places. "I want you to buy it."

Doesn't this seem outlandish?! Jeremiah himself says, "You all are going in for a whole generation of captivity." Despite that, God comes, and He says, "Pay a price for the land that you are losing right now, for the time will come when the land will be occupied yet again, and there will be houses there, there will be fields there, and there will be a harvest there." God is saying to us that we need to pay a price for what may look ridiculous. It may appear to run counter to the facts. Would there be a people who would buy it anyway? Would there be a people of God willing to pay such a price?

That The Excellence Of The Power May Be Of God

Notice this interesting detail: Jeremiah has to put the deed to the land he buys in an earthen container. We also have to take the promises of God - the title deed to the destiny that God has called us to - and put it in our own earthen container- which is inside of us.

2 Corinthians 4:7 *But we have this treasure in earthen vessels, that the excellence of the power may be of God and not of us.*

This is why the whole story happens the way it does for Abraham and Sarah. God calls Abram to be the father of many nations because he's barren - that the excellency might be of God and not of man.

We see this clearly in their story, and this brings us back to a new source of fear for them. Ishmael is born when Abraham was 86. Now, 13 years later, Isaac is still not born. A lot of time has passed, even after Ishmael. The promise comes again, "You're going to have a son with Sarah." Abraham laughs, and he says, "Oh, that Ishmael might live!" Sometimes, we reject what God has really called us to, and we place our hopes in the thing that we've birthed ourselves, which is like an imitation of what God wants to do.

We say, "Oh God, would you just bless this thing?", but it's not what God has ordained. We can find ourselves asking God to bless the Ishmael in our lives. He's saying, "No, there is still going to be an Isaac", but we laugh. Later, when Sarah discovers she's going to have a child, she also laughs! Then, God comes and says, "Why did you guys laugh?"

We have to come to the place where we acknowledge, "I just didn't have enough faith." When we acknowledge that and say, "Lord, forgive my unbelief! Lord, would you put faith in me for all that You desire to bring forth in my life?"

I believe there is yet another reason why Abraham and Sarah are fearful at this point in their lives. Between the first time they deny they are husband and wife and the second time, the story with Lot and Sodom and Gomorrah happens. What an overwhelming event for anyone to see! Sometimes, we observe situations, experience events, or see great shakings that can really confound us. Many have been sidelined because of that. We have to make sure that our faith stands secure. Our faith cannot fail because someone else fell. Abraham and Sarah find themselves shaken up after the whole incident with Lot.

God says to Abimelech, "Restore Sarah and let Abraham pray for you." I believe the earth is crying out to us, saying, "Would you speak into my life? Would you say that which God has birthed within you?"

Now Isaac Can Come Forth!

As soon as Abraham and Sarah are restored to who they are supposed to be, Isaac is born the next year. He is born "at that set time" God had all along. We can feel like we are barren. We can feel like we have a prophetic word, but we have to be careful not to allow ourselves to set a time clock in our own minds.

We must simply stand on the word. All those years later, God says, "Here's Isaac!" Isaac's name means laughter. The name itself reminds us that we don't have the full measure of faith for all that God wants to do. Despite our "laughter" or lack of faith, God does it anyway, and God finally gives us the faith to believe and stand on His promises. May we be like Abraham and Sarah when they brought forth Isaac. Like them, may we know that God brought us through to receive the promise.

It Happens Again!

Once again, a generation later, because of famine, Isaac and Rebekah go to a place called Gerar. They leave the place where they lived. Unlike Abraham and Sarah, this happens after their children are born. This has special meaning and gives us fresh revelation for our lives.

Jacob and Esau have been born and are grown. Abraham and Sarah deny they are husband and wife before Isaac is born, but Isaac and Rebekah deny it after their children are born. What does this speak of to us? I believe it speaks of the various stages in our walk where we are at-risk of losing our identity because of fear. One stage, just like Abram and Sarai, is at the beginning. We can lose our identity in Christ right at the beginning.

The second story of Abraham and Sarah denying their identity happens right before a birthing. We need to be careful when we are in a season of birthing! We might be on the verge of birthing our "Isaac" and suddenly deny who we really are.

The third stage of our walk that denial often happens is in a place of maturity. When we have already birthed something and our ministry is mature, we can hear the voice of the enemy saying, "You've already had your time. You've done what God called you to do. You can sit back now." Some of you may be young when you are reading this, but you're not always going to be young!

I believe that this word is going to stick with you, and that you are going to have a watch over your minds. I believe that you are going to recognize when the voice of the enemy comes, because when you're older, sometimes that is what the voice of the enemy says.

I want everyone to be encouraged that the Lord's purposes in your life stand. Whether you are young, in your middle years, or in your later years, you are called to be who the Lord created you to be!

It's Not Over Until It's Over

I love the story of Anna and Simeon: they both continued pressing into their destiny in their old age. Anna was in the temple every single day, and it was her privilege to see the baby Jesus brought in with her own eyes. Anna was able to declare, "Now, I've seen it! Now, I can prophesy into this situation. This is that which I've been waiting to see." Simeon had the same testimony as Anna: "Now, I'm ready to go. This Child is the fulfillment of all that God has spoken."

We can read Christian biographies of great men and women of God! I like the fact that Smith Wigglesworth was advanced in years when he went into the ministry. God is never done. There are always great things to do ahead.

I have a good friend who is in her 90's. She is an awesome prophet of God with a powerful voice in the Body of Christ. For decades, she traveled, taught, and prophesied. Today, she's old and rather infirm, but her mind and spirit are fully there! Whenever I teach in the church, I tell her that I want her in the room, in order that she might speak up when God says something to her. I let her know that I want her to pray for my Bible classes. I always want her to share the wisdom and truth of what God places on her heart.

You are not "done" when you are old! If you were done, you would be dead. God takes us home when our work is done. If you are still here, you still have something great ahead!

I like sharing about one of Jesus' parables that teaches us that the longer we've been in the Kingdom of God, the more effective we can become. God does a cumulative work within us.

These three stories of identity crisis in the Book of Genesis remind us that whatever stage we are in, there is a risk of being conformed to the world. When we conform out of fear, we risk losing our identity in Christ. The world senses we have failed them when we aren't true to our God-given destiny. They proclaim in their hearts, "Why have you done this to us?"

Let The People Of God Arise!

I think of Romans 8 when I see the Pharaoh and the king of Gerar both saying, "Why did you do this to us?"

Romans 8:19 *For the earnest expectation of the creation eagerly waits for the revealing of the sons of God.*

Can you imagine that these worldly leaders actually wanted Abraham and Sarah, and Isaac and Rebekah, to be who they really were? The people of the earth may sound like they don't want believers to take their place, but they are "eagerly waiting" for the sons of God to be revealed! They may not be able to articulate it clearly, but they want us to be who God intends.

Deep in their hearts, they know that they need us. This is the exact posture I take with people who seem to dislike Christians. I know because I was one of them. I was the number-one debater against Christianity in high school. I couldn't stand it! Now, it's easy to see that I was the number-one candidate to get saved.

Even when people say things that sound like they are rejecting my message, I remind myself that they really want the gospel. They just don't know it yet! To me, the more opposed they seem, the closer they are to accepting Jesus.

They really care and are full of conviction. Indifference is more problematic than opposition. God says in Revelation 3:15-16, "I would that you were hot or cold, because you're lukewarm, that's a no-go for Me." When people are vocally against the things of God, like Saul before he became Paul, I think, "Hmm, we're going to pray now. We're going to see a great harvest."

The earth is crying out for Christians to embrace their identity. A few verses later, in

Romans 8:22, we read: *For we know that the whole creation groans and labors with birth pangs together until now.*

Looking at the news and all of the calamities around us, we see a lot of groaning and travailing and a lot of pain. For what? The creation groans that we would be the manifested sons of God; that we would rise up and be who we are supposed to be!

After Isaac and Rebekah began to live openly again as husband and wife, there was an immediate change. With Abraham and Sarah, Isaac could be born (after their second identity crisis.) With Isaac and Rebekah, a great harvest resulted from their identity being restored.

Genesis 26:12 *Then Isaac sowed in that land, and reaped in the same year a hundredfold; and the LORD blessed him.*

That land speaks of destiny. When Isaac and Rebekah were finally themselves, they experienced great fruit and blessing.

The True You

We can see that these three stories are all about the same thing and are all found in the Book of Genesis. Why? It's because we need to know who we really are! In each of these stories, they had to bring forth fruit and be who they really were. Why? The world was suffering. In each case, it was the world that declared, "Why are you doing this to us?" When we are not honest about who we are, who the Lord created us to be, we cannot bring forth in the same dimension. We cannot walk in the same dimension of power.

It's interesting that in Abraham and Sarah's story, there was actually some truth to their lie.

Genesis 20:12 *But indeed she is truly my sister. She is the daughter of my father, but not the daughter of my mother; and she became my wife.*

We can claim that we aren't who God wants us to be because of a variety of accurate reasons and difficulties. There can be some truth, or even a lot of truth, in the hardships that we have wounded us or prevented us from walking in the dimension that God intends. With that said, I believe God is a God of restoration. I don't know what's ahead for each one of you, but I know that the Lord is faithful to complete that which He started in us. I think about what Paul says to the Ephesian elders in Acts 21. When he is on his way to be martyred, Paul gathers all the Ephesian elders together, and he says, "The word of the Lord keeps coming, and the Holy Spirit says everywhere I go that bonds and afflictions await me."

His message was not, "You're awesome! You have an enjoyable life ahead." No. The message was really hard! Nevertheless, Paul was able to say, "None of these things move me!" God wants to put a, "But none of these things move me," in your spirit today. When news comes that a Christian leader fell, we can feel bad for them and let him who is spiritual restore such a one. Oh, that we would be ones who are spiritual! Instead of allowing other people's mistakes to blow our minds, let's settle it in our heads - people aren't perfect. People make mistakes all the time. If we are only going to press in when everyone else is onboard and doing the right thing, we won't be able to accomplish all that the Lord would have us to do.

There are many stories from persecuted countries where believers are in really difficult circumstances. Believers might end up in jail. For decades. Survivors have been asked what was it like. They were all alone, and it was grueling and gruesome. What was it like? The answer was, "Oh, it was like a honeymoon. I got to be with Jesus every day." Wow! It's not contingent on natural circumstances. Do we want things to be good and life to run smoothly?

Yes, absolutely; I pray that there would be favor and good things in store for all of us; but, there are also hard circumstances. Hard things will come to each one of our lives. What will we do then? I believe we have in our spirit, like Paul, "But none of these things move me." We will overcome if we are willing; if we allow Him to move in that dimension; if we say, "I'm not going to be controlled by the fear of man."

1 John 4:18 *There Is no fear in love; but perfect love casts out fear, because fear involves torment. But he who fears has not been made perfect in love.*

When we know that God loves us, we can have full confidence.

A Joshua Hour!

We are living in a Joshua hour! In Joshua 1, when the word comes to Joshua, there has been a lot of wondering in the wilderness.He is given an opportunity to take hold of those things that were missed previously. Likewise, we have another chance to take the Promised Land in our lives. The Book of Acts has been around for 2,000 years. Now, there is going to be a people who press in for the whole thing, just like in the day of Joshua.

The Israelites had spent 40 years wandering around in the same location. Do you feel like that sometimes in your own spiritual life? Do you feel like you've been going around in circles? I have often felt that way in my own life, and I think, "Lord, let us break out of that! Lord, let us press in. Let us not have to wander." The reason the people of Israel had to wander was because an evil report came. There was a good report that said, "We can do it!", but the evil report came and said, "Oh, no, there are some giants in the land. Taking hold of the Promised Land might be too hard for us to do. We're like grasshoppers in their sight." Sadly, the people chose to believe that lie. God said, "Okay, then, you're going to wander until you can overcome that mindset."

God is looking for a people who will say, "We can do it!" Isn't that what King David did? Before David was king, he was little brother David, the youngest of eight siblings. David had a courageous spirit. It was this courageous posture that David took when all of his older brothers were in the battle. Jesse, his dad, said, "Go ahead and bring them some bread and cheese."

It was because of this assignment that David had the opportunity to kill Goliath. Again, it's like Stephen in Acts 6.

David and Stephen were not given glorious, glamorous jobs, but they made of them what the King of Kings would have them do. David went, and he delivered the bread and cheese - because we still have to do those things we've been assigned to do - and he discovered the entire army of Israel was in total bondage to a giant named Goliath.

He took a look at this - the younger brother who nobody thought anything about - and he said, "This doesn't make any sense! What is going on here?" You know how the story ends: David took Goliath down and said, "How dare you, you uncircumcised Philistine!"

God is raising up people who no one else would look at twice. There are great Kingdom exploits to be accomplished, and God is raising up unexpected and overlooked people to do them. Maybe no one thought Stephen would be the first martyr or preach such a powerful, convicting sermon that people had to plug their ears; no one expected little David to slay Goliath, but they accomplished it through the power of the Holy Spirit! God wants to do that in our lives.

Joshua also took this posture: it was time to do what Moses could not accomplish. Now, they could now take hold of the Promised Land.

Joshua 1:2 *Moses My servant is dead. Now therefore, arise, go over this Jordan, you and all this people, to the land which I am giving to them--the children of Israel.*

That's the voice of the Holy Spirit in this hour saying, "Arise!" Cross over some places that haven't been crossed over yet. To do it, you need to authentically be who God has destined and ordained you to be.

The Power Of Identity

The first question that God would ask us is, "Are you the sibling or are you the spouse?" Are you going to be who God called you to be? Are you going to be someone powerful and unique? Will you apprehend that for which you've been apprehended?

God is raising up a new generation of Samsons who let their hair grow again. This generation will say, "I might have lost my vision for a while, but now I am going to cause more damage to the kingdom of darkness than it has ever imagined. The enemy thought he had me wrapped up, bound up, and in bondage, but watch this!"

God is raising up a new generation of people like Paul, Barnabas, Matthew, Mark, Luke, and John: people who say, "I can do this! I can be unusual and unique like Smith Wigglesworth. I can be someone who has never been seen before on this earth!" He wants to raise each one of us up to have courage - a very good courage - to step up higher and take land that's never been taken. He will give us courage to be different: people who boldly choose not to be conformed to this world; people who don't deny we are married to Jesus; people who say, from the Song of Solomon, "I am my Beloved's and my Beloved is mine."

It's the power of identity.

Lord Jesus, I pray that You are going to cause us to be saturated by your Holy Spirit. May these words sink deep within us. Cause us to be a generation who would rise up and be everything that You have called us to be. Let us no longer be conformed to this world, but transformed by the renewing of our minds. Lord, cause the renewing of our minds to occur! Cause our hair to grow again, Lord Jesus. Cause us to have an understanding of who the Delilahs are in our life. Cause us to be those who say, "I am the spouse! I am not the sib

Make It Personal

1. What role has fear played in your life? What do you fear? Be as specific as possible.

2. What are the lies you've heard relating to your identity and also your purpose?

3. When you consider that the world is waiting for us to be who we truly are, and to accomplish what God has purposed us for, and that in the absence of us apprehending both, there is a curse upon them, how does that affect you? What do you think about it? What emotions are stirred?

CHAPTER 4

God's Lost And Found!

In the last few chapters, we laid a foundation, and now it's time to build on it. We saw that Jesus knew who He was. As we looked at the Gospel of John, we discovered that each of the seven "I AM" statements that Jesus made produced a manifestation in the supernatural. I believe God wants us to walk in the supernatural realm, but we first must know who we are. Among other Kingdom business, we need to know who we are in order to fulfill the Great Commission and bring in the lost. Just as Jesus spoke to Peter, He is making us into fishers of men!

We looked at some unique personalities in the Bible and saw how each one of us is a unique creation, formed in the womb for a unique destiny. We also discovered that the enemy is an identity robber. When Samson allowed his uniqueness to be cut off, we observed how he was almost completely destroyed. We talked about some of the things that can distort our identity and discovered that fear is one of the greatest identity robbers.

When we feel afraid, I believe we need to stop in that moment, ask ourselves what our fear is, and perhaps write it down. Then, we need to look at our fears and address them with the Scriptures. The enemy wants us to keep our fears in the dark because that is where he likes to use his "smoke and mirrors." The very things that we may be afraid of can subtly work within us to create a distortion.

We also addressed the pressure of conformity that is so prevalent today. We observed in the stories of Abraham and Sarah (twice!) and Isaac and Rebekah that they denied their true identities. In reality, they were husband and wife, but they chose to pose as brother and sister. This spoke to us about the points in our walk with Christ when we are most at-risk of denying who we really are: the beginning of our walk with Him, right before God wants to birth something in our lives, or when we've reach maturity and have already birthed something. We need to be on guard. We need to be vigilant through all the seasons of life to never lay down that which God has called us to do. Throughout the Scripture, we see that the Lord desired to raise up a radical people. He still does today!

There Is More!

Philippians 3:12-13 *Not that I have already attained, or am already perfected; but I press on, that I may lay hold of that for which Christ Jesus has also laid hold of me. Brethren, I do not count myself to have apprehended; but one thing I do, forgetting those things which are behind and reaching forward to those things which are ahead,*

The Lord would have us be those who reach into the future and take hold of that which God has ordained. I love Jeremiah 1:5, where God spoke to Jeremiah and told him that He ordained him from the womb.

There are messages, miracles, and breakthroughs that you have been ordained to bring that are still in your future. That means we can't let those things that are behind us cause us to be deflected from the purposes that are ahead of us. Rather, we must be those who have an ever-expanding vision and revelation for the future.

Proverbs 29:18 *Where there is no revelation, the people cast off restraint; But happy is he who keeps the law.*

70

A more exact translation for the word revelation is progressive vision. The phrase people cast off restraint speaks of dwelling carelessly. In this season of the Great Harvest, we don't want to be wandering around, dwelling carelessly; but instead, we need to have a progressive vision! We need to live our lives with purpose in this great hour of prophetic destiny.

There is a great revelation in the story of the manna. The manna came supernaturally to Israel, and they were told, "You have to gather this every single day. That which you gathered yesterday is no longer good for today." The Lord wants to stir us up and have us say, "Lord, I need your manna for today. I need the present word - the prophetic word - that You are speaking today. What would you have me do today?" I think it is significant that the Bible explains that on the sixth day, they had to gather a double portion because on the seventh day, the Sabbath, there was to be no gathering.

I believe that we are living in the sixth day; that we are living in a season where God is saying, "Today, in this season, you have to gather double!" In the past, it may have been good enough to have a lesser level of revelation. The Lord is saying, "No, you need a deeper revelation; you need to have enough for the days ahead."

I love that the Bible mentions this manna is meant to feed your whole household. What does that mean? It means that God puts people around us, and He would have us attain a level of revelation where we have enough to both sustain ourselves and feed other people.

Nehemiah 8:10 *Then he said to them, "Go your way, eat the fat, drink the sweet, and send portions to those for whom nothing is prepared; for this day is holy to our Lord. Do not sorrow, for the joy of the LORD is your strength."*

The Lord would have us be busy gathering fresh revelation so that we would have enough to give to people who have nothing prepared for them: the Great Harvest! People are looking for someone with an answer for today. Let us be those who consume all that the Lord has for us to such an extent that we have an overflow for all who are hungry for a touch from God.

When believers walk in their true identity, it positively affects the entire earth. Let us not forget, however, that when we don't walk in who we really are, it also impacts the earth. The world becomes plagued, and it becomes a very barren place indeed!

God's Lost And Found!

The entire Gospel of Luke revolves around seeking that which is lost. Luke 15 is the centerpiece chapter, but let's also look at Luke 19, so we can understand what it means to seek that which is lost.

Luke 19:1-2 *Then Jesus entered and passed through Jericho. Now behold, there was a man named Zacchaeus who was a chief tax collector, and he was rich. Jesus entered and passed through Jericho.*

In this season of the Great Harvest, we must lose our preconceived notions about who is or who isn't a candidate to be saved. Here is "Exhibit A": Zacchaeus. He is a chief publican, a despised class of people in that society. He is rich! Many of us would say, "Oh, doesn't the Bible say that there are not many rich who come into the Kingdom?" Yes, but there are some. We must be walking in our true identity in order to touch the rich, the poor, the people who are beloved, the people who are hated, the people who do good, and the people who do evil! Zacchaeus is an unlikely candidate for the Gospel.

Luke 19:3 *And he sought to see who Jesus was, but could not because of the crowd, for he was of short stature.*

Zacchaeus is a short man who literally cannot see Jesus. This story historically took place this way, but it is also a picture to us. There all sorts of reasons why people have not yet gotten to Jesus, but I believe that many sincerely want to get there. It is between each individual and God if they ultimately reject Jesus once they see Him. Until that point - until they are dead and standing before Jesus - I am going to believe they are yet to get to Jesus. God's calling on each one of us is: Get the people to Jesus!

Luke 19:4 *So Zacchaeus ran ahead and climbed up into a sycamore tree to see Him, for He was going to pass that way.*

Zacchaeus had heard Jesus was coming by, and he thought, "I'm really short. I can't see, so I'll climb into a tree." We don't know how many people have run ahead of us and are, figuratively, sitting in trees, waiting for us to pass their way! God wants to change our mindset. When we go places, when we are in the marketplace, or when we are out and about, we would begin to look and ask the Lord, "Who's up in the trees? Who's waiting to have an encounter with You?"
There is no time for us to be shy and say to ourselves, "Oh, they don't really want to hear." We must believe, "Yes, they do want to hear!" They are in the trees, and they are waiting. This is what Zacchaeus was doing that day in the tree.

Luke 19:5 *And when Jesus came to the place, He looked up and saw him, and said to him, "Zacchaeus, make haste and come down, for today I must stay at your house."*

We need to be looking up, too! Just as Jesus knew Zacchaeus' name, we need to get personal with people. We are not going to meet people in our place of comfort; rather, we will meet them in their place of comfort and in their territory. Theirs!

Luke 19:6-9 *So Zacchaeus made haste and came down, and received Him joyfully. But when they saw it, they all complained, saying, "He has gone to be a guest with a man who is a sinner." Then Zacchaeus stood and said to the Lord, "Look, Lord, I give half of my goods to the poor; and if I have taken anything from anyone by false accusation, I restore fourfold." And Jesus said to him, "Today salvation has come to this house, because he also is a son of Abraham."*

Verse 10 is the key verse for the entire Gospel of Luke. It sums it all up!

Luke 19:10 *For the Son of Man has come to seek and to save that which was lost.*

This is to be our call, too. Seeking and saving the lost is what we are here in this life to do. Our identity is intimately wrapped up in this most important call.

Matthew 4:19-20 *Then He said to them, "Follow Me, and I will make you fishers of men." They immediately left their nets and followed Him.*

Although Peter and Andrew were both ultimately called to be apostles, they had very different personalities. The Lord is saying the same thing to us, regardless of our call, and regardless of our personality: "If you will follow Me, then I will make you into fishers of men." It is God's desire to accomplish that in each one of our lives. The key, however, is to follow Jesus and to do the things that He did.

Think about this: It takes all kinds of people to reach all kinds of people. This is why identity comes into play! You may be able to speak to a person no one else can speak to because you are uniquely you. Will there be some people who will not have an ear to hear what you have to say? Yes, but I believe there will be someone else who will be able to speak into their lives. It takes all different types to seek and to save that which is lost.

I believe the Lord is enabling us to accomplish this most monumental of tasks. He is causing us to appreciate the uniqueness of each individual. In our hearts today, let us determine to open our eyes and look into the trees and ask, "Lord, who do You want me to speak to? Who do You want me to minister to? Who can I pour out to that perhaps no one else can reach?" God will most certainly use our uniqueness to fulfill this great call.

The Lost Sheep, The Lost Coin, And The Lost Son

Now, let's take a look at Luke 15.

Luke 15:1-32 *Then all the tax collectors and the sinners drew near to Him to hear Him. And the Pharisees and scribes complained, saying, "This Man receives sinners and eats with them." So He spoke this parable to them, saying: "What man of you, having a hundred sheep, if he loses one of them, does not leave the ninety-nine in the wilderness, and go after the one which is lost until he finds it? And when he has found [it], he lays it on his shoulders, rejoicing. And when he comes home, he calls together his friends and neighbors, saying to them, 'Rejoice with me, for I have found my sheep which was lost!' I say to you that likewise there will be more joy in heaven over one sinner who repents than over ninety-nine just persons who need no repentance.*

Or what woman, having ten silver coins, if she loses one coin, does not light a lamp, sweep the house, and search carefully until she finds it? And when she has found it, she calls her friends and neighbors together, saying, 'Rejoice with me, for I have found the piece which I lost!' Likewise, I say to you, there is joy in the presence of the angels of God over one sinner who repents."

Then He said: "A certain man had two sons. And the younger of them said to his father, 'Father, give me the portion of goods that falls to me.' So he divided to them his livelihood. And not many days after, the younger son gathered all together, journeyed to a far country, and there wasted his possessions with prodigal living. But when he had spent all, there arose a severe famine in that land, and he began to be in want. Then he went and joined himself to a citizen of that country, and he sent him into his fields to feed swine. And he would gladly have filled his stomach with the pods that the swine ate, and no one gave him anything.

But when he came to himself, he said, 'How many of my father's hired servants have bread enough and to spare, and I perish with hunger! I will arise and go to my father, and will say to him, "Father, I have sinned against heaven and before you, and I am no longer worthy to be called your son. Make me like one of your hired servants." ' And he arose and came to his father. But when he was still a great way off, his father saw him and had compassion, and ran and fell on his neck and kissed him. And the son said to him, 'Father, I have sinned against heaven and in your sight, and am no longer worthy to be called your son.'

But the father said to his servants, 'Bring out the best robe and put it on him, and put a ring on his hand and sandals on his feet. And bring the fatted calf here and kill it, and let us eat and be merry; for this my son was dead and is alive again; he was lost and is found.' And they began to be merry.

And he said to him, 'Your brother has come, and because he has received him safe and sound, your father has killed the fatted calf.' But he was angry and would not go in. Therefore his father came out and pleaded with him. So he answered and said to his father, 'Lo, these many years I have been serving you; I never transgressed your commandment at any time; and yet you never gave me a young goat, that I might make merry with my friends.

But as soon as this son of yours came, who has devoured your livelihood with harlots, you killed the fatted calf for him.' And he said to him, 'Son, you are always with me, and all that I have is yours. It was right that we should make merry and be glad, for your brother was dead and is alive again, and was lost and is found.' "

In this chapter, we see the stories of three things that were lost: the lost sheep, the lost coin, and the lost son. In each of the cases, there is ownership in the story.

The Lost Sheep

There is a shepherd, and he has 100 sheep, but one of his sheep is gone. The story continues, and we see this shepherd leave the 99 to pursue the one lost sheep. When the shepherd finds this lost sheep, he puts it on his shoulders with joy. Shoulders, in the Scriptures, speak of strength and authority. The Lord wants us to recognize how important every single person is. This refers to the lost who don't know Jesus, but it is also for believers whose unique identity may be lost. Perhaps that which God has called them to be has been lost.

I believe that the Lord is calling each one of us to places of leadership and places of authority. The Lord is giving us big shoulders - not in order to look puffed up and important - because there are people who need you to lift them up, put them on your shoulders, and take them back into their place in the Body of Christ. This is the point of the story: every single person is important! We can't look out and say, "Well, most everyone is here; that's good." No!

We notice who is there and who isn't there. We take account of the people. We look into the trees and say, "Lord, what do You want me to see? This person wasn't here. That person seemed discouraged." The Lord is saying, "Go and find them! Put them on your shoulders."

The Lost Coin

In the story of the lost coin, a woman has ten coins - again, it's ownership. This work of seeking and finding is not for someone else to do. It's for us to do! Looking at Ephesians 4, where it describes the five-fold ministry - the apostle, the prophet, the evangelist, the pastor, and the teacher - we read that their purpose is to equip the saints, so that the people can do the work of the ministry. We must all be able to rise up and say, "I'm going to take ownership of this. This is my neighborhood - I'm going to take ownership."

A woman has ten coins, and she realizes one is lost. Again, we must recognize the value in every person. It's not enough have nine coins. No, one of these valuable items has been cast aside. She lights the lamp and sweeps the place until she finds it. We must light the lamp of the Word of God in our lives. We should have so much of the Word of God in us that we are a light! The Scriptures remind us not to put our light under a bushel; instead, we're to let our light shine so that those around us can see it. There is great darkness upon the earth; we urgently need to be people who shine forth as bright lights.

The story of the lost coin teaches us an important lesson. When someone doesn't know the Lord yet, or someone knows the Lord but doesn't recognize their value, that is the time for our light to burn the brightest. It is not acceptable to say, "Well, I'm sorry they are depressed." No, we say, "I'm going to bring the light and sweep the place clean to find that person where they are."

Isaiah 60:1-3 *Arise, shine; For your light has come! And the glory of the LORD is risen upon you. For behold, the darkness shall cover the earth, And deep darkness the people; But the LORD will arise over you, And His glory will be seen upon you. The Gentiles shall come to your light, And kings to the brightness of your rising.*

May each one of us arise and shine in this unique and important moment in history!

The Lost Son

The final story, which only occurs in the Gospel of Luke, is the story of the prodigal son - the lost son. We learn that the lost son comes from the Father's house, speaking to us of a believer who has lost their way. This wayward son decides he wants his inheritance now; he takes it and leaves his Father's house. Soon, it all turns into a fiasco! The prodigal son spends all of his money and ends up living with pigs. How tragic to see how far he falls.

The Scripture, though, shows us the beautiful heart of the Father. The Father is poised, looking for his son. He runs to him as soon as he sees him coming. As Jesus looked for Zacchaeus, the father looks for his son. The son is still a far way off when the Father sees him. We must do the same. Let us look for people who are hungry, who are lost, who are desperate for a place at the Father's table. There is room for everyone in our Father's house.

I believe in the importance of our God-given uniqueness. Each individual sees different things and knows different people. The variety of these elements come into play for the unsaved to come into the Kingdom. I also believe there will be those who used to be a part of the Kingdom who no longer are. They may feel rejected and like they have failed. They matter to the Father. They need to matter to each one of us as well. Let us take ownership of all that the Lord puts in our hand. May we not allow a single one in our view be left out of the massive net of God's love.

Make It Personal

1. You've been fashioned to reach people far from God and bring them to Jesus. How is your willingness to embrace your true identity affected when you consider you've been uniquely designed with others in mind?
2. What aspects of your identity can you rethink now and, instead of being uncomfortable with them, begin to appreciate how God has made you?

3. It takes all kinds of people to reach all kinds of people. Who can you pour out to that maybe no one else can reach?

CHAPTER 5

Thank God For Barnabus!

In "God's Lost and Found," we saw that every single believer and every single nonbeliever matters to the Lord. Everyone matters to the Lord; each person has great value.

I want to share a story with you in the Scriptures that beautifully depicts this truth. I think it is one of the greatest stories in the Bible. It has profoundly touched my life. I want to look at it carefully with you, so that it can weave its truth into your spirit for a lifetime. This story involves four well-known people in the Bible: Paul, Barnabas, Mark, and Peter. As we delve in, we will see how truly unique and vital each person is.

John Mark Joins The Ministry Team Of Barnabas And Saul

Acts 12:25 *And Barnabas and Saul returned from Jerusalem when they had fulfilled their ministry, and they also took with them John whose surname was Mark.*

In this verse, we are introduced to a man named John Mark. This is the same person who later writes the Gospel of Mark. As we come across this scene in the Scriptures, we discover how these people interact.

I enjoy having this birdseye view. I love the Book of Acts and the epistles for this reason. We can see how real church life is. It's not glossed over for us. It's not depicted without problems. No! These aren't accounts where everyone is holy and well-mannered. Instead, we see actual personalities and issues. In Acts 12, the first missionary journey has begun, and it is powerful! In the next chapter, we read about the first prophetic presbytery.

Acts 13:1-3 *Now in the church that was at Antioch there were certain prophets and teachers: Barnabas, Simeon who was called Niger, Lucius of Cyrene, Manaen who had been brought up with Herod the tetrarch, and Saul. As they ministered to the Lord and fasted, the Holy Spirit said, "Now separate to Me Barnabas and Saul for the work to which I have called them." Then, having fasted and prayed, and laid hands on them, they sent them away.*

It is here that we observe the Holy Spirit speaking through the prophets and teachers that it was time to separate Barnabas and Saul out and send them to the mission field. It is awe-inspiring to hear a call like this. The reality is, regardless of our callings, we still have personalities; we still have conflicts among people; there are still issues. We see all of these aspects as this story unfolds.

Acts 13:5 *And when they arrived in Salamis, they preached the word of God in the synagogues of the Jews. They also had John as their assistant.*

The story continues, and we find that John Mark has become Paul and Barnabas' assistant. The word assistant is the same word that we often translate as deacon. The ministry team has expanded to three.

John Mark is there to help them because this is an enormous undertaking, and they need his help. While Paul and Barnabas are busy preaching the Gospel and leading many people to the Lord, John Mark can accomplish the necessary day-to-day tasks of life.

John Mark's role is not an easy one. Let's consider what it must have been like for them at that time. Stephen has been martyred. They are forced to leave Jerusalem because the persecution causes them to scatter. The Lord uses this, of course, to open the door to preach to the Gentiles. This is not according their plan, though! This is God's plan. They find themselves in an unfamiliar place.

Somehow, they manage to lessen the load by taking John Mark with them, but it is still a very hard missions trip. There's no welcoming committee, no friends to relax with, and no nice accommodations. If you've been on a missions trip before, you know that they are almost never easy. Don't get me wrong: they are worth every bit of effort, and you come back better for it. I think every believer should go on at least one missions trip. The truth is, though, they bring out the worst in you. You don't sleep; there's not good food; you might get sick. I don't want to scare you away from missions trips, because they are amazing experiences, where you get to see lives changed and miracles performed in front of your eyes. But...they are hard!

This one is harder still, because they are risking imprisonment and even their lives. None of this is easy-breezy. When we look at the story of John Mark in the Scriptures, we discover that he comes from a wealthy family. John Mark is used to a pretty comfortable life. Well, now John Mark is on the mission field with Paul. Paul has a very focused personality; he is all about the business of bringing the Gospel. Don't you just love Paul? I do! I especially like the story in Acts 20 about the time Paul had been preaching for hours.
A man named Eutychus is sitting at the third story window; he falls asleep, tumbles out, and dies. Paul essentially says, "I'll be right back." Paul proceeds to pray for Eutychus, bringing him back to life! Then, Paul pops back up to the Upper Room and continues teaching until morning. We can definitely conclude that Paul has a strong, determined personality.

Paul And Barnabas

God, in this prophetic presbytery in Acts 13, says, "Paul, come forward. I'm sending you on the mission field, but I'm sending you with a partner: Barnabas." There may not be two people who are more different than Paul and Barnabas. I love it! You might be sitting next to someone, or ministering next to someone, who is so different from you that, apart from the Kingdom, you may never have had the opportunity to stand with them. Isn't that beautiful? God is using our differences so that we might see the fullness of what God wants to do in our midst. It is going to take a multi-membered Body to touch the earth.

There they are: Paul and Barnabas, and now John Mark. Paul is raising people from the dead and continues on teaching. Barnabas, though, is completely different. He is just as Kingdom-minded, but it manifests in a different way. Even Barnabas' name proves to be indicative: Barnabas means "The son of Consolation." He is a really nice guy.

He's the one in a crowd who can resolve conflicts. He really cares about people. Paul, though, is focused and thinking, "Oh my, there are thousands and thousands of people who need to get saved. We don't have any time to mess around. If Eutychus dies, I'm just going to raise him back to life. We're not going to skip a beat." Barnabas is a much friendlier type of person. Both are equally needed! We are not all the same!

When I was 19-years-old, I met my husband. He came into the church that I was attending. I was already someone who would teach and preach. He had never seen this before! He came from a Catholic background, and he had only seen men preach in the church. We began to date, and very shortly thereafter, he asked me to marry him. I said, "Oh! Well, I know what God has called me to do, and I'm not going to be your typical wife, cooking and doing all of that stuff! I know what God has called me to do." He said, "I know, and that's what I love about you." So, almost 40 years later, we've been married 38 years, and he's my biggest fan. It's like he knew that this was not only my call; it was his, too! I've gone on the mission field, and he's totally fine with it. We have two adult daughters now, and six grandkids. He has a very mellow personality that works perfectly with mine. You couldn't have two of me, or we would be at each other all the time! It takes all kinds.

uh-Oh, John Mark Leaves The Team!

Act 13:13 *Now when Paul and his party set sail from Paphos, they came to Perga in Pamphylia; and John, departing from them, returned to Jerusalem.*

Verse 13 introduces the conflict. We have our ministry trio: Paul (super-focused), Barnabas (friendly and resolves conflict), and John Mark (new on the scene and from a rich family). It would be easy to read that verse and think, "Oh, I guess John Mark departed", but we get a glimpse later of what this is all about. To summarize, the road trip is more than John Mark could take. He doesn't have the fortitude, and he leaves the mission field. I think he probably said something like, "This is for the birds! I'm ready to go back home."

We need to move forward two chapters in Acts to see how this situation resolves.

Acts 15:36 *Then after some days Paul said to Barnabas, "Let us now go back and visit our brethren in every city where we have preached the word of the Lord, [and see] how they are doing."*

In this passage, we get a glimpse into how situations like this can happen. We see Paul being classic, ultra-focused Paul. Paul is saying, "Okay, we just came back from our mission trip and told all our fellow believers in Antioch all about it. That was great. I think we have rested enough! Let's go again!"

A Great Disagreement Arises

Acts 15:37 *Now Barnabas was determined to take with them John called Mark.*

This is a big deal. God wants us to understand that even those, like John Mark, who have stepped aside from the ministry, might be candidates to step right back in again. Barnabas, with his unique personality and giftings, understands that. Barnabas is determined to not allow John Mark to be left in a place of failure and regret.

Acts 15:38-41 *But Paul insisted that they should not take with them the one who had departed from them in Pamphylia, and had not gone with them to the work. Then the contention became so sharp that they parted from one another. And so Barnabas took Mark and sailed to Cyprus; but Paul chose Silas and departed, being commended by the brethren to the grace of God. And he went through Syria and Cilicia, strengthening the churches.*

"But Paul...." That is a phrase we can stop and consider. Paul is not the same as Barnabas. He doesn't see things the same way regarding John Mark. To Paul, John Mark is a point of potential trouble: someone who could create a hindrance. To Barnabas, John Mark is worth it.

Barnabas understands the truth that every single person matters to the Lord and to the Kingdom. Barnabas makes the right decision in restoring John Mark to the ministry. Later, we will see that Paul eventually comes to the same conclusion. The good news is that the ministry doubles: Paul and Silas make a good team, and Barnabas and John Mark make a good team.

The important lesson to take from Barnabas' example is that people are worth fighting for. He knows that he can carry John Mark on his shoulders (like the shepherd with his lost sheep) and bring him back to the place that he is destined to be. Barnabas is willing to speak up on John Mark's behalf.

Can you imagine the great Apostle Paul saying, "No, I don't want John Mark to travel with us." That would very difficult for John Mark to hear about! That could make many of us say, "Well, forget it. I just won't do it. The Apostle Paul doesn't think much of me." I love that Barnabas, the encourager, has the wisdom and compassion to say, "John Mark is worth fighting for, and I'll fight for this." Acts 15 says that the contention - the fight - is so strong that it causes a split into two ministry teams.

Really?! Those things happen in the Book of Acts? Yes, they do! It takes about twelve years for Paul to admit that Barnabas had been right.

Oh, How Easy It Is To Forget Where We Have Come From

Before we look at the conclusion of this story, let's roll the story back several years to when Paul got saved in Acts 9. The Church doesn't want to touch him with a ten-foot pole! Even Ananias, who is sent by God to pray with him, has to say, "Lord, are You sure? Isn't this the guy who has been killing all the Christians? Really?

You want me to go pray for this guy?" Of course, the Lord did, and Ananias obeys the Lord and prays for Paul. Paul gets saved, but we learn that the Church doesn't want to accept Paul. I think it is amazing and strangely encouraging that even Kingdom "greats" experience times of rejection. Let's discover who exactly took Paul under his wing!

Acts 9:26-27 *And when Saul had come to Jerusalem, he tried to join the disciples; but they were all afraid of him, and did not believe that he was a disciple. But Barnabas took him and brought him to the apostles. And he declared to them how he had seen the Lord on the road, and that He had spoken to him, and how he had preached boldly at Damascus in the name of Jesus.*

Barnabas becomes Paul's spokesperson! The Church doesn't want to receive Paul, but Barnabas says, "No, this man is worth fighting for. " The same character trait in Barnabas that wants to restore John Mark is demonstrated previously in Paul's life. Paul must have forgotten this in his driving passion to be about the Kingdom business… but a realization does dawn on him twelve years later.

Paul's Change Of Heart

Colossians 4:10 *Aristarchus my fellow prisoner greets you, with Mark the cousin of Barnabas (about whom you received instructions: if he comes to you, welcome him)*

Paul has finally come to the conclusion that Barnabas was indeed right all those years earlier about John Mark. John Mark is back in the picture. I love that Paul could say, "I was wrong. Barnabas was right. John Mark is valuable. Please welcome him if he comes to you."

2 Timothy 4:11 *Only Luke is with me. Get Mark and bring him with you, for he is useful to me for ministry.*

What a poignant statement. This is written at the end of Paul's life in his final letter to Timothy, his son in the faith. Paul is saying that he is all alone, except for Luke, but he asks that Timothy come and bring John Mark with him! Paul says that John Mark is useful to him in the ministry.

There is nothing more important than people. When we say, "Oh God, I want to be who You've called me to be. I want to be the unique vessel that You have made me to be," we have to understand the purpose in it has to do with people. We want to be everything God has destined us to be so that people can be touched and restored.

Barnabas sees hidden value in John Mark. It's as if John Mark is a lost coin. Barnabas says, "I'm going to take ownership of this, even though John Mark made a mistake when he turned back." Barnabas wants to recover John Mark's value. What is so beautiful about this story is that the story doesn't end there. We see that John Mark, when he writes the Gospel of Mark, includes a story that is only found in his gospel. Imagine if Barnabas hadn't contended for John Mark. We might not have the Gospel of Mark! Let's look at that story that is only told in the Gospel of Mark.

A Special Story Only Appearing In The Gospel Of Mark

Mark 14:27-31 *Then Jesus said to them, "All of you will be made to stumble because of Me this night, for it is written: 'I will strike the Shepherd, And the sheep will be scattered.' But after I have been raised, I will go before you to Galilee." Peter said to Him, "Even if all are made to stumble, yet I will not be." Jesus said to him, "Assuredly, I say to you that today, even this night, before the rooster crows twice, you will deny Me three times."*

Mark 14:66-72 *Now as Peter was below in the courtyard, one of the servant girls of the high priest came. And when she saw Peter warming himself, she looked at him and said, "You also were with Jesus of Nazareth." But he denied it, saying, "I neither know nor understand what you are saying." And he went out on the porch, and a rooster crowed. And the servant girl saw him again, and began to say to those who stood by, "This is [one] of them." But he denied it again. And a little later those who stood by said to Peter again, "Surely you are [one] of them; for you are a Galilean, and your speech shows [it]." Then he began to curse and swear, "I do not know this Man of whom you speak!" A second time [the] rooster crowed. Then Peter called to mind the word that Jesus had said to him, "Before the rooster crows twice, you will deny Me three times." And when he thought about it, he wept.*

Less than a day passes before Jesus' prophecy over Peter is fulfilled. This experience could have ruined Peter. No doubt Peter feels like a complete failure and that his place in the Kingdom is not recoverable. Jesus does something that only Mark records. I love this. I believe Mark is chosen to record it because he really understands, having experienced failure himself.

Whatever we have been through impacts our uniqueness. Our mistakes feed into it; our successes feed into it; our wounds feed into it. As we allow God to redeem each part of our lives, we can speak into the lives of people we would never have been able to otherwise. There are all sorts of people who have made mistakes! There are all sorts of people who have walked where you have been before, and they are waiting, just like Zacchaeus, for someone who will notice them. They are waiting for someone who has a word to speak into their life, born out of the experiences they have had. I believe that this is what Mark is doing because Peter shared this story with Mark.

People may say, "What are you doing? You should be doing this or that! You should make a lot of money or do this instead!" Perhaps some of you are called to make a lot of money; do it! That's what you're called to do. For others, the call of God can truly break the mold! I have a missionary friend who was called to China over 50 years ago.

At the time of his call, everyone was against it! China wasn't open then. You couldn't get into China! People asked him, "Are you crazy?! Couldn't you do something better? Something you can actually DO?" All sorts of commentary can come into our lives on why we shouldn't be doing what God has called us to do.

In response to this criticism, my missionary friend said, "No. Here's what I'm going to do. I'm going to go to Hong Kong, which is open and which borders China. I'm going to be there. That way, the minute the door to China opens, I will get in there! Since they speak Chinese in Hong Kong, I will learn that language." He had his eyes fixed on "China, China, China!" That's all he could see. None of it made sense to those around him, but he left with a one-way ticket. 50 years later, he has undoubtedly changed the destiny of millions in the nation of China.

When we are doing that which God has called us to do, the anointing is there; the favor is there; the abilities are there. The miracles are there because we're busy about the Father's business. We must take hold of the form that God intends for us to have. There's a freedom that comes in no longer being conformed to what everyone else thinks we ought to be.

There is a radical people that God is raising up in this hour. They are radical because they are who God made them to be. That, my friend, is exactly what the enemy fears: a bold people pressing the darkness back and bringing the light of the Kingdom to an entire generation.

I can imagine an interaction between Peter and John Mark. Maybe Peter takes John Mark aside, because Peter is mentoring John Mark, and says, "I also made a terrible mistake once. Let me tell you my story..." It is John Mark who explains it to us, as he writes what I believe to be one of the most beautiful passages in the Bible.

Mark 16:1-7 *Now when the Sabbath was past, Mary Magdalene, Mary the mother of James, and Salome bought spices, that they might come and anoint Him. Very early in the morning, on the first day of the week, they came to the tomb when the sun had risen. And they said among themselves, "Who will roll away the stone from the door of the tomb for us?" But when they looked up, they saw that the stone had been rolled away--for it was very large. And entering the tomb, they saw a young man clothed in a long white robe sitting on the right side; and they were alarmed. But he said to them, "Do not be alarmed. You seek Jesus of Nazareth, who was crucified. He is risen! He is not here. See the place where they laid Him. But go, tell His disciples--and Peter--that He is going before you into Galilee; there you will see Him, as He said to you."*

Jesus specifically wants Peter included, despite Peter's great failure. Jesus knows how terrible and disconnected Peter feels after fulfilling Jesus' prophecy. Jesus seeks Peter out and sends the messenger to tell the ladies, "Go get the disciples. Go get Peter." Why? Can you imagine how horrible Peter would feel when he finds out that the disciples are all with Jesus because Jesus has indeed risen? Jesus wants to make sure that Peter isn't excluded.

How much more so do we need to do the same thing? Of course, Jesus is perfect, but we've all failed! Who are we to exclude anyone in any way? I understand that there is a need for church discipline. There can be short seasons when someone isn't a part of ministry. I am not talking about that. We need to be looking for people who are wounded on the sidelines and bring them back to their place of significance.

It thrills me that Mark gets to write this story, that the Holy Spirit quickens Peter's story to Mark. It was John Mark who had turned back, and he no doubt found comfort in this story. He had a great, personal desire to impart its truth. Mark and Peter both experienced grace and healing. Paul also experienced it after Barnabas took him under his wing, despite his history as the great persecutor of the Church.

Peter, Mark, and Paul were all carried on the shoulders of another. May we be people who carry others on our shoulders and ensure that no one is overlooked.

You Have Been Called As An Ambassador & You Have A Ministry Of Reconciliation!

2 Corinthians 5:17-21 *Therefore, if anyone is in Christ, he is a new creation; old things have passed away; behold, all things have become new. Now all things are of God, who has reconciled us to Himself through Jesus Christ, and has given us the ministry of reconciliation, that is, that God was in Christ reconciling the world to Himself, not imputing their trespasses to them, and has committed to us the word of reconciliation. Now then, we are ambassadors for Christ, as though God were pleading through us: we implore you on Christ's behalf, be reconciled to God. For He made Him who knew no sin to be sin for us, that we might become the righteousness of God in Him.*

This is the call of God on each one of us. We are ambassadors for Christ and His great Kingdom! The first thing we need to do is speak a word of reconciliation to ourselves. If you feel that, for any reason, you are not a full candidate to be used by God, be encouraged today! You are a new creation, and you have received reconciliation.

Your identity matters because YOU are an ambassador for Christ. You speak people's languages that no one else speaks. If you're called to be an ambassador to France, we would certainly hope you speak French! If you're called to be an ambassador to Argentina, we would hope you speak Spanish. God calls us to be ambassadors to different people groups and different situations. Why? It's because you speak their language. You are going to be the one to say, "Zacchaeus, today I must meet with you in your house! I must come to the place of your comfort - to the place where you live."

The Importance Of Each Person

I cannot finish this chapter without talking about Philip the evangelist. Philip has an amazing ministry opportunity in Samaria, and multitudes are getting saved! The people are listening to every word that Philip is saying. Then, the Lord speaks to him...

Acts 8:5-8 *Then Philip went down to the city of Samaria and preached Christ to them. And the multitudes with one accord heeded the things spoken by Philip, hearing and seeing the miracles which he did. For unclean spirits, crying with a loud voice, came out of many who were possessed; and many who were paralyzed and lame were healed. And there was great joy in that city.*

Acts 8:26-40 *Now an angel of the Lord spoke to Philip, saying, "Arise and go toward the south along the road which goes down from Jerusalem to Gaza." This is desert. So he arose and went. And behold, a man of Ethiopia, a eunuch of great authority under Candace the queen of the Ethiopians, who had charge of all her treasury, and had come to Jerusalem to worship, was returning. And sitting in his chariot, he was reading Isaiah the prophet. Then the Spirit said to Philip, "Go near and overtake this chariot." So Philip ran to him, and heard him reading the prophet Isaiah, and said, "Do you understand what you are reading?"*

And he said, "How can I, unless someone guides me?" And he asked Philip to come up and sit with him. The place in the Scripture which he read was this: "He was led as a sheep to the slaughter; And as a lamb before its shearer is silent, So He opened not His mouth. In His humiliation His justice was taken away, And who will declare His generation? For His life is taken from the earth." So the eunuch answered Philip and said, "I ask you, of whom does the prophet say this, of himself or of some other man?" Then Philip opened his mouth, and beginning at this Scripture, preached Jesus to him. Now as they went down the road, they came to some water. And the eunuch said, "See, [here is] water. What hinders me from being baptized?" Then Philip said, "If you believe with all your heart, you may."

And he answered and said, "I believe that Jesus Christ is the Son of God." So he commanded the chariot to stand still. And both Philip and the eunuch went down into the water, and he baptized him. Now when they came up out of the water, the Spirit of the Lord caught Philip away, so that the eunuch saw him no more; and he went on his way rejoicing. But Philip was found at Azotus. And passing through, he preached in all the cities till he came to Caesarea.

Think about this passage of Scripture. It is all about the importance of one single believer. Philip is in the middle of a tremendously successful ministry trip, and the Lord says, "I have a person - a single person - over here. Go and talk to him." Philip goes immediately at the Lord's call, and, through his obedience, the Ethiopian eunuch enters the Kingdom. Did you notice that Philip does not return to his previous place of ministry in Samaria?

Philip is translated into another place of ministry, and we never see him back there again. Why do we learn this detail? Ministry is not about fame, successful "numbers," and giant stadiums filled with people. No! Someone like Philip achieves that, and yet God says, "I want you to go to the one.

I have a lost sheep over here. I want you take that which I have put into your life, that which I have imparted to you, and I want you to put that one on your shoulders. I want you to light a lamp and look for that which is of value that has been lost. It's somewhere in there - I'm sure it is! I want you to have your eyes open and search for the lost son who wants to return to his Father's house." That is the redemption story of the Scriptures!

May we be people who are willing to stand up on behalf of those who have made mistakes but want to be restored! May we help them rise up and once again serve in their Kingdom purpose!

Make It Personal

1. Read 2 Corinthians 5:17-21 again. Your God-given mission is as an ambassador, as if God is pleading to people through you, "Be reconciled..." With whom will you plead? Will it be to your own self first? If so, what words of grace and reconciliation would you speak to your own heart and mind?

2. Who is the John Mark in your realm of influence? Do you know someone who is useful for service, of great importance, but who has been sidelined for some reason? What will you do about it?

CHAPTER 6

The Sword Of The Lord and of Gideon!

I cannot go any further on the topic of identity without bringing in the story of Gideon. I pray that this story will resonate with you and that you will say, "Lord, show me who I am! I am going to be who I am called to be because I will know who that is. Lord, I know that when I am truly who I am supposed to be, You are going to back it up with that which You have called me to do!"

It's By God's Spirit!

Zechariah 4:6 *So he answered and said to me: This is the word of the Lord to Zerubbabel: 'Not by might nor by power, but by My Spirit,' says the Lord of hosts.*

As the message of identity has been rumbling around in my spirit for years, I have treasured this scripture from Zechariah. I believe we must not do things in our own strength any longer. If we try to fulfill our call in our own strength, we are not going to accomplish anything! Instead, we will become completely fatigued. In this hour, we find ourselves in a battle on every side. Every front is being attacked. We must know how to fight these battles!

2 Corinthians 10:4 *For the weapons of our warfare are not carnal but mighty in God for pulling down strongholds.*

The Story Of Gideon

Through the story of Gideon, we can understand how mighty our warfare can be. Let's begin by noticing how Gideon is mentioned in the "Heroes of the Faith" in Hebrews 11.

Hebrews 11:32-34 *And what more shall I say? For the time would fail me to tell of Gideon and Barak and Samson and Jephthah, also [of] David and Samuel and the prophets: who through faith subdued kingdoms, worked righteousness, obtained promises, stopped the mouths of lions, quenched the violence of fire, escaped the edge of the sword, out of weakness were made strong, became valiant in battle, turned to flight the armies of the aliens.*

These verses in Hebrews 11 immediately follow the accounts of the "heroes" of faith, such as Abraham, Isaac, Jacob, and Joseph. Gideon is right there on this list! Gideon's name appears because he is a powerful person in God who accomplishes his destiny. Gideon rises up at a critical time to fulfill his unique call. I want to look at how he does that because the Lord wants each one of us to rise up in the same way!

Gideon's story is found in Judges 6-8. When you study the heroes of the faith, one aspect that is common to all of them is this: they rise up in the midst of trouble. Heroes don't appear on the scene when everything is going well; they show up in the midst of turmoil and despair.

Judges 6:1 *Then the children of Israel did evil in the sight of the Lord. So the Lord delivered them into the hand of Midian for seven years,*

The name Midian means stress and strife. Do you sometimes feel that you've been delivered into a place of stress and strife? That is where the children of Israel find themselves in this story.

Judges 6:2 *And the hand of Midian prevailed against Israel. Because of the Midianites, the children of Israel made for themselves the dens, the caves, and the strongholds which are in the mountains.*

The Israelites go into hiding! Have you ever felt forced into hiding? Have you figuratively gone to live in a cave because of the enemy? We find ourselves in situations that have been of our own making, but, in reality, it is the destruction of the enemy in our lives.

Judges 6:3 *So it was, whenever Israel had sown, Midianites would come up; also Amalekites and the people of the East would come up against them.*

The enemy joins forces against Israel as they begin to sow. Instead of one difficult circumstance, we come up against multiple ones. The enemies join together. Enemies collaborate against us when we have sown something! Inevitably, when a Kingdom purpose is about to come forth - when good seeds have been planted - the enemy comes to wreak havoc.

Judges 6:4-5 *Then they would encamp against them and destroy the produce of the earth as far as Gaza, and leave no sustenance for Israel, neither sheep nor ox nor donkey. For they would come up with their livestock and their tents, coming in as numerous as locusts; both they and their camels were without number; and they would enter the land to destroy it.*

The Enemy Is Out To Get You!

John 10:10 *The thief does not come except to steal, and to kill, and to destroy. I have come that they may have life, and that they may have it more abundantly.*

Let's not fool ourselves! The enemy is out to destroy us. That is what John 10:10 tells us. However, that verse also tells us that Jesus has come that we might have life more abundantly. It is the tension between these two forces that is always at play in our lives on this earth. Jesus gives us new life, but the enemy is determined to destroy every purpose ordained for our lives.

But Victory Can Be Ours!

1 Corinthians 15:57 *But thanks be to God, who gives us the victory through our Lord Jesus Christ.*

Gideon shows us keys to enable us to prevail victoriously.

Judges 6:6 *So Israel was greatly impoverished because of the Midianites, and the children of Israel cried out to the Lord.*

Israel experiences this domination by the Midianites for seven years. In this season of difficulty, the Lord does a great work of preparation within them. Likewise, I believe, in our seasons of struggle, the Lord does a monumental work within us. It is in the midst of the furnace of affliction that we begin to cry out to Him.

Judges 6:11 *Now the Angel of the Lord came and sat under the terebinth tree which was in Ophrah, which belonged to Joash the Abiezrite, while his son Gideon threshed wheat in the winepress, in order to hide it from the Midianites.*

Remember: the children of Israel are all living in caves, and they are all afraid of the enemy. However, they must eat something, so we discover a man named Gideon threshing wheat. Gideon has chosen his position carefully; he is threshing wheat in the winepress to keep it out of the Midianites' hands.

Judges 6:12 *And the Angel of the LORD appeared to him, and said to him, "The Lord is with you, you mighty man of valor!"*

What an unexpected greeting! In my own mind, I would create a different dialog. "Oh Gideon, you poor, pathetic thing. Look at you! You are hiding in the wine press. You will not amount to much." That is definitely not the message from the Lord. The Lord sees Gideon as a mighty man of valor!

The Lord also says to each of us, "The Lord is with you. You are a mighty person of valor." Even if you are in hiding, trying to keep yourself safe, the Lord desires to do something powerful within you.

Even as the Lord spoke to Gideon, I believe that God is speaking to many modern-day Gideons in this season. The enemy may think, "Oh, I've got them! God's people are so ineffective. They're hiding in caves!" What the enemy doesn't realize is that the Lord is doing a powerful work in His people. Threshing in the winepress is going on unbeknownst to the enemy. The enemy may see us as ineffectual, but the Lord sees us as mighty people of valor.

Judges 6:15-16 *So he said to Him, "O my Lord, how can I save Israel? Indeed my clan is the weakest in Manasseh, and I am the least in my father's house." And the Lord said to him, "Surely I will be with you, and you shall defeat the Midianites as one man."*

We can clearly see that it isn't Gideon's physical strength that causes the Lord to use him. In fact, Gideon is saying, "Why me? Where are my qualifications? I don't feel or look the part. The circumstances around me aren't looking good either." The Lord simply responds with a reassurance that He will go with him.

Romans 8:31 *What then shall we say to these things? If God is for us, who can be against us?*

Gideon's name means, "somebody who cuts down." In the Old Testament, names speak of a person's prophetic destiny. At first, Gideon certainly isn't acting like his destiny. Gideon hasn't been cutting anything down, but nonetheless, Gideon is called prophetically from birth to be one who cut down the enemy. Gideon doesn't have the confidence yet to walk in that destiny. Instead, he says, "Who am I? Nothing looks right here, God. Even amongst my brothers, I'm the least of everyone. Why would You say this to me?" There is a processing that must take place within Gideon.

Some Things Just Have To Go!

Judges 6:25-26 *Now it came to pass the same night that the Lord said to him, "Take your father's young bull, the second bull of seven years old, and tear down the altar of Baal that your father has, and cut down the wooden image that is beside it; and build an altar to the Lord your God on top of this rock in the proper arrangement, and take the second bull and offer a burnt sacrifice with the wood of the image which you shall cut down."*

Isn't this fascinating!? God requests the offering of a 7-year-old bull. Remember: they had been tormented by the Midianites for seven years. God wants Gideon to burn the 7-year-old bull on top of the wood from the idol that he instructs him to cut down.

The Lord has Gideon beginning to walk in his destiny of cutting down! Only God can use our times of difficulties to help propel us into our destinies!

Romans 8:28 *And we know that all things work together for good to those who love God, to those who are the called according to [His] purpose.*

This part of Gideon's story teaches us that the difficulties we've been through are about to become an offering to the Lord. It's going to be a complete work! I love that it says, "tear down the altar of Baal that your father has." Much of our oppression can involve generational bondages. There are habits and mindsets that we can bring with us, even after our salvation. For example, someone may have a fear of stepping out because of something that happened in their home as a child. There are countless possibilities of what we may carry that the Lord never intended. The Lord is saying, "It's time to cut those things down!"

In this hour of breakthrough for your destiny, I love that He says, "You're going to build an altar on top of this rock." This is all going to happen on the foundation of Jesus, our Rock!

Judges 6:33-35 *Then all the Midianites and Amalekites, the people of the East, gathered together; and they crossed over and encamped in the Valley of Jezreel. But the Spirit of the Lord came upon Gideon; then he blew the trumpet, and the Abiezrites gathered behind him. And he sent messengers throughout all Manasseh, who also gathered behind him. He also sent messengers to Asher, Zebulun, and Naphtali; and they came up to meet them.*

When we take hold of the charge of God on our life, the enemy prepares for battle. The enemy camps in the valley, waiting for Gideon. Don't miss the key phrase: "But the Spirit of the Lord came upon Gideon." We cannot do this in our own strength!

Gideon walks in the Spirit, and he has a prophetic anointing. The verse declares that Gideon blows the trumpet; trumpets in Scripture speak to us of prophetic voices. Gideon also gathers others around him who have the same vision.

We must walk in the Spirit and have the Word of the Lord in our mouths. Like Gideon, we need to blow the trumpet in this hour and bring those with us who have the same vision.

Confirming The Call

Judges 6:36-40 *So Gideon said to God, "If You will save Israel by my hand as You have said--look, I shall put a fleece of wool on the threshing floor; if there is dew on the fleece only, and it is dry on all the ground, then I shall know that You will save Israel by my hand, as You have said." And it was so. When he rose early the next morning and squeezed the fleece together, he wrung the dew out of the fleece, a bowlful of water. Then Gideon said to God, "Do not be angry with me, but let me speak just once more: Let me test, I pray, just once more with the fleece; let it now be dry only on the fleece, but on all the ground let there be dew." And God did so that night. It was dry on the fleece only, but there was dew on all the ground.*

What does this mean? I often hear people talk about fleeces, but I don't sense that we have accurately comprehended the meaning. Gideon is saying, "There can't be any chance for coincidence." If we are going to walk in what the Lord has called us to, we must believe it without reservation.

Where we have misapplied the fleece concept is when we try to get God's "stamp of approval" on what we want, as opposed to confirming what we sense the Lord is saying to us. It is a subtle, but important, difference. Gideon isn't saying to the Lord, "Hey, Lord, here is what I would like to do. Let's see if you are okay with this." No, Gideon is saying, "I think I have heard this word from You, and it has great implications. Lord, I want to make sure this truly came from You."

James 1:6-8 *But let him ask in faith, with no doubting, for he who doubts is like a wave of the sea driven and tossed by the wind. For let not that man suppose that he will receive anything from the Lord; he is a double-minded man, unstable in all his ways.*

We must not waver in our resolve to fulfill the purposes of the Lord. Before we go into battle, we must settle in our hearts why the Lord has created us and called us.

The New Testament teaches us that prophetic utterances need to be confirmed by the mouth of two or three witnesses.

1 Corinthians 14:29 *Let two or three prophets speak, and let the others judge.*

2 Corinthians 13:1b *...By the mouth of two or three witnesses every word shall be established.*

When we hear from the Lord, it is necessary to have confidence that God Himself has spoken. With confirmation, we are assured that we haven't heard our own (or a prophet's) random thought. Rather, God has spoken, and He wants us to run with it!

1 Timothy 1:18 *This charge I commit to you, son Timothy, according to the prophecies previously made concerning you, that by them you may wage the good warfare,*

Confidence in our call is essential because it is going to take strength and courage to defeat the enemy. The enemy comes at us with every bit of discouragement and all the lies that he can muster. Satan is the accuser of the brethren, and he does not want to see us flourish in our true identity and destiny.

Gideon is saying, "I have to be sure." The Lord responds, "Settle it in your heart. Gideon, you are about to go into battle, and you will prevail."

Camp Beside A Well!

Judges 7:1 *Then Jerubbaal (that is, Gideon) and all the people who were with him rose early and encamped beside the well of Harod, so that the camp of the Midianites was on the north side of them by the hill of Moreh in the valley.*

Gideon has another name - Jerubbaal. The name means "contender of Baal." Recall that Gideon's father sets up an altar to Baal. Baal is the idol that Gideon's enemy worships. The Lord calls Gideon to not only cut down the idol, but also to contend with the idolatry that is a stronghold in that place. First, Gideon and all the people who are with him, need to rise up and pitch their tent by the well. This speaks to us of our need to drink deeply of the Holy Spirit and His Word.

John 7:38 *He who believes in Me, as the Scripture has said, out of his heart will flow rivers of living water.*

This is where we need to make our camp. There is nothing more important than having daily communion with the Holy Spirit and consuming the Word as our bread. In this great Kingdom hour, we need to pack ourselves with His Word, so God can quicken it to us by the power of the Holy Spirit.

More Things Have To Go!

Judges 7:2 *And the LORD said to Gideon, "The people who are with you are too many for Me to give the Midianites into their hands, lest Israel claim glory for itself against Me, saying, 'My own hand has saved me.'*

This is not a picture of God eliminating people - that goes against everything we have been learning. God wants to add people to His kingdom, not subtract them. This is a picture of what God is doing within us. Some components within us need to be eliminated. As the Lord cuts things out, it might seem like we have gone from a big place to a small place. However, the Lord is actually making us more pure in order to expand us again with the ingredients He knows we need.

Philippians 1:6 *Being confident of this very thing, that He who has begun a good work in you will complete it until the day of Jesus Christ;*

We can rest in confidence that the One who has made us and loves us has a magnificent design that He is bringing forth. Do not feel discouraged in a season of diminishment. Rest assured that expansion is coming.

Fear Must Go!

Judges 7:3 *"Now therefore, proclaim in the hearing of the people, saying, 'Whoever is fearful and afraid, let him turn and depart at once from Mount Gilead.' " And twenty-two thousand of the people returned, and ten thousand remained.*

One of the greatest obstacles in fulfilling all that the Lord has called us to is fear. Gideon's story displays this truth clearly. The largest cut from Gideon's army is those who are fearful. The Lord says, "You mighty person of valor. It is amazing what I have called you to do."

When fear comes, we may think to ourselves, "I'm afraid of what will happen and how others may react. I'm afraid of the consequences. I'm afraid of failing." Therefore, the Lord desires to cut those places of fear out of us.

Picture: inside of you, there are 32,000 parts. A significant portion of those parts can be fear. Fear has to go: fear of man, fear of the future, fear of lack of money, fear of ill health, fear of what other people think. Whatever the fear is, it can be one of the biggest influences inside of us. God wants to get rid of it. That's why, in Gideon's story, He says, "Whoever has fear has to go." It is the largest cut.

2 Timothy 1:6-7 *Therefore I remind you to stir up the gift of God which is in you through the laying on of my hands. For God has not given us a spirit of fear, but of power and of love and of a sound mind.*

I love how the New Testament echoes the message that we hear in the Old Testament. Paul is saying, "Timothy, you are awesome! Great things are ahead. Remember the prophetic impartation of gifts you received. Stir them up, but don't be afraid! Remember: fear isn't from God, for He has given us power, love, and a sound mind."

Fear is in opposition to the unique call the Lord has given to each of us. The Lord is coming by His grace to help us eliminate fear in our lives.

We Must Correctly Consume The Word Of God

Judges 7:4-7 *But the Lord said to Gideon, "The people are still too many; bring them down to the water, and I will test them for you there. Then it will be, that of whom I say to you, 'This one shall go with you,' the same shall go with you; and of whomever I say to you, 'This one shall not go with you,' the same shall not go."*

So he brought the people down to the water. And the Lord said to Gideon, "Everyone who laps from the water with his tongue, as a dog laps, you shall set apart by himself; likewise everyone who gets down on his knees to drink."

And the number of those who lapped, putting their hand to their mouth, was three hundred men; but all the rest of the people got down on their knees to drink water. Then the Lord said to Gideon, "By the three hundred men who lapped I will save you, and deliver the Midianites into your hand. Let all the other people go, every man to his place."

Here we see the second elimination process that the Lord commands. Gideon has eliminated those who have fear, but now there is something else that must go. There are still 10,000 people after the fearful ones leave. The Lord instructs Gideon to bring them down to the water. He reveals to Gideon that there are two ways that the people might drink the water. One way is acceptable; the other way requires the people to pack up and go home.

What does this mean to us today? The Lord is saying that how we consume the water is critically important. The water is a picture to us of the Word of God. God is speaking to each one of us today, and He is saying, "You cannot fulfill the destiny on your life by sheer giftedness and charisma. You cannot fulfill it by being connected or in the right place at the right time." The Lord will certainly use our gifts and give us divine connections, but what is important is how we consume the Word of God.

Every aspect of our ministry is impacted by this. We must not just operate out of our giftedness; we must ensure we have the substance to properly accompany it. That substance becomes part of the anointing that we carry.

We Need Vision!

Gideon is commanded to dismiss those who do not drink the water in the prescribed way. Why is it unacceptable to kneel down to drink?

It's because, as they would kneel, they would put their faces in the water, and they would not have any vision. By contrast, those who scoop up the water in their hands and bring it to their mouths are able to keep looking forward. They retain their vision as they drink!

Proverbs 29:18 *Where there is no vision, the people perish: but he that keeps the law, happy is he.*

The Lord wants us to consume His Word in such a way that increases our vision. We must drink deeply of the water of the Word in this hour.

Think about all the stories in the Scriptures about eyesight. It is remarkable to study those who keep and those who lose their eyesight.

1 Corinthians 10:11 *Now all these things happened to them as examples, and they were written for our admonition, upon whom the ends of the ages have come.*

A great example is the story of Eli and young Samuel found in 1 Samuel 3.

1 Samuel 3:1-5 *Now the boy Samuel ministered to the Lord before Eli. And the word of the Lord was rare in those days; there was no widespread revelation. And it came to pass at that time, while Eli [was] lying down in his place, and when his eyes had begun to grow so dim that he could not see, and before the lamp of God went out in the tabernacle of the Lord where the ark of God was, and while Samuel was lying down, that the Lord called Samuel.*

And he answered, "Here I am!" So he ran to Eli and said, "Here I am, for you called me." And he said, "I did not call; lie down again." And he went and lay down.

This passage notes that the Word of the Lord is rare and that Eli's eyes have grown dim. It is a picture to us of not having a deep life in the Word which produces sharp vision. Observe what happens in the story: the next generation, Samuel, is hearing God's voice, but he doesn't recognize it yet. Eli, the High Priest, should be able to instruct Samuel that it is the Lord who is speaking to him. Instead, Eli tells Samuel to go back to sleep. What a tragedy! It has to happen multiple times before Eli recognizes that the Lord may be speaking to Samuel. God forbid we, in this hour, be people who somehow communicate to this generation to go back to sleep! No, it's time to awaken people to the voice of the Lord. May we be people whose vision never dims. It matters how we consume the Word.

Bring Your Food And Your Trumpet

Judges 7:8 *So the people took provisions and their trumpets in their hands. And he sent away all the rest of Israel, every man to his tent, and retained those three hundred men. Now the camp of Midian was below him in the valley.*

Gideon's army is instructed to take food and their trumpets with them. Likewise, we need to eat the food of the Spirit in order to be sustained. We must carry our own food. Just like the manna in the wilderness, everyone needs to gather it for their own household. They are also commanded to have their trumpets with them.

The trumpet is a type to us of the prophetic voice. We must carry our spiritual food and the prophetic voice with us at all times. We need them both!

Judges 7:12 *Now the Midianites and Amalekites, all the people of the East, were lying in the valley as numerous as locusts; and their camels were without number, as the sand by the seashore in multitude.*

We know that God's ways are not our ways. Simultaneous to the enemy gathering an innumerable number to come against Gideon, the Lord cuts Gideon's forces down from 32,000 to 300. None of it makes sense in the natural, but that is often how the Lord works!

2 Corinthians 4:7 *But we have this treasure in earthen vessels, that the excellence of the power may be of God and not of us.*

Oh, that we would know the excellency is of Him and not of us! We are so much stronger when we allow the Lord to cut away and remove from us what doesn't belong there by His design.

An Encouraging Report!

Judges 7:13-14 *And when Gideon had come, there was a man telling a dream to his companion. He said, "I have had a dream: To my surprise, a loaf of barley bread tumbled into the camp of Midian; it came to a tent and struck it so that it fell and overturned, and the tent collapsed." Then his companion answered and said, "This is nothing else but the sword of Gideon the son of Joash, a man of Israel! Into his hand God has delivered Midian and the whole camp."*

Gideon goes into the enemy's camp. I think it's awesome that the enemy knows Gideon's name and exactly where he comes from! The enemy recognizes Gideon's call, even if Gideon doesn't fully comprehend it yet.

Judges 7:15 *And so it was, when Gideon heard the telling of the dream and its interpretation, that he worshiped. He returned to the camp of Israel, and said, "Arise, for the Lord has delivered the camp of Midian into your hand."*

The Word of God and the prophetic voice can sustain us when we accept that the enemy is actually afraid of us. The Lord will make the enemy our footstool. The enemy is aware of this. May a fresh level of encouragement come to us as we meditate on this.

It's Time To Do This!

Judges 7:16 *Then he divided the three hundred men into three companies, and he put a trumpet into every man's hand, with empty pitchers, and torches inside the pitchers.*

The Lord is instructing us to take trumpets - the prophetic - with us. We are the empty pitchers! We must make sure that we have a light inside of us. It is the light of His Word and the light of the Holy Spirit.

Matthew 5:14 *You are the light of the world. A city that is set on a hill cannot be hidden.*

Isaiah 60:1-3 *Arise, shine; For your light has come! And the glory of the Lord is risen upon you. For behold, the darkness shall cover the earth, And deep darkness the people; But the Lord will arise over you, And His glory will be seen upon you. The Gentiles shall come to your light, And kings to the brightness of your rising.*

Judges 7:17-18 *And he said to them, "Look at me and do likewise; watch, and when I come to the edge of the camp you shall do as I do: When I blow the trumpet, I and all who are with me, then you also blow the trumpets on every side of the whole camp, and say, 'The sword of the Lord and of Gideon!'"*

This passage contains a tremendous truth! God is going to use our uniqueness. The Lord can do everything all by Himself, but He gives us the privilege to participate and partner with Him. He says, "It's not just 'the sword of the Lord,' but it's also 'the sword of Gideon.'" The Lord is saying that He wants to use us as vessels. How profound that we actually get to share in the victory. What grace! What glory! What love!

We can have great influence in our lives because people are looking at us. That's why Gideon says, "Look at me and do likewise." If we would rise up and be who God has called us to be, others are going to look at us and say, "Wow! If that person can do it, then I can do it, too." The Lord is looking for forerunners who will say, "I'm going to do it!"

Matthew 11:11-12 *Assuredly, I say to you, among those born of women there has not risen one greater than John the Baptist; but he who is least in the kingdom of heaven is greater than he. And from the days of John the Baptist until now the kingdom of heaven suffers violence, and the violent take it by force.*

I enjoy what Jesus says here about John the Baptist: there has been no greater prophet. Wow! This wild-looking guy, out in the wilderness, is preparing the way of the Lord!

The Lord is looking for people who would rise up, take their spiritual food and the prophetic with them, and be a great light shining in a very dark earth. The world is searching and crying out for people to bring light into their circumstances.

Judges 7:19-21 *So Gideon and the hundred men who were with him came to the outpost of the camp at the beginning of the middle watch, just as they had posted the watch; and they blew the trumpets and broke the pitchers that were in their hands. Then the three companies blew the trumpets and broke the pitchers--they held the torches in their left hands and the trumpets in their right hands for blowing-- and they cried, "The sword of the Lord and of Gideon!" And every man stood in his place all around the camp; and the whole army ran and cried out and fled.*

Gideon divides the 300 men into three groups of 100. What a beautiful picture we see when everyone stands in his place around the camp.

1 Corinthians 12:20-21 *But now indeed there are many members, yet one body. And the eye cannot say to the hand, "I have no need of you"; nor again the head to the feet, "I have no need of you."*

Each one of the 300 men are important. Each one is needed. When everyone stands in their proper place, all the enemy host flees. Why? It's because the trumpets are blown and the light shines; the people are where they are supposed to be.

The Lord would say, "Where is your place? How have I made you? What is the purpose that I have given you?" The Lord desires to reveal these answers to us!

You have a particular place to take: that's why it is the sword of the Lord and of Gideon. There is the the sword of the Lord, and there is your sword, too. There is something unique that the Lord has called you to be and to do. It is one of the greatest mysteries in creation that God would have us be part of the best thing He ever let down from heaven.

Others Will Follow Your Lead

Judges 7:22-24 *When the three hundred blew the trumpets, the Lord set every man's sword against his companion throughout the whole camp; and the army fled to Beth Acacia, toward Zererah, as far as the border of Abel Meholah, by Tabbath. And the men of Israel gathered together from Naphtali, Asher, and all Manasseh, and pursued the Midianites. Then Gideon sent messengers throughout all the mountains of Ephraim, saying, "Come down against the Midianites, and seize from them the watering places as far as Beth Barah and the Jordan." Then all the men of Ephraim gathered together and seized the watering places as far as Beth Barah and the Jordan.*

As we step out in battle, claiming who we really are in Christ, I believe that others are going to follow and join us. They will be willing to be in the battle when they see victory has already begun. I think the challenge to each one of us is, "Will you be a forerunner? Will you be like Gideon?" I sense that the enemy is quaking in his boots, fearful that any one of us might rise up and be who God has called us to be.

Judges 8:1 *Now the men of Ephraim said to him, "Why have you done this to us by not calling us when you went to fight with the Midianites?" And they reprimanded him sharply.*

What does this verse mean? When the forerunners have the victory, many will be sorry that they hadn't possessed the courage from the start. We don't want to live with the regret of missing out on all that the Lord desires for us. We want to be those who say, "I want the fullness of what You have for me, Lord. I don't want to look back later and realize that I could have done more for the Kingdom."

Have you ever had the opportunity to be with someone who is dying? It is both sad and fascinating to listen to their regrets. We want to live life with no regrets at the end! May we not look back and think, "Oh, I wish I had done this; I wish I had seen my true purpose in a clearer focus."

Judges 8:4-8 *When Gideon came to the Jordan, he and the three hundred men who were with him crossed over, exhausted but still in pursuit. Then he said to the men of Succoth, "Please give loaves of bread to the people who follow me, for they are exhausted, and I am pursuing Zebah and Zalmunna, kings of Midian." And the leaders of Succoth said, "Are the hands of Zebah and Zalmunna now in your hand, that we should give bread to your army?" So Gideon said, "For this cause, when the Lord has delivered Zebah and Zalmunna into my hand, then I will tear your flesh with the thorns of the wilderness and with briers!" Then he went up from there to Penuel and spoke to them in the same way. And the men of Penuel answered him as the men of Succoth had answered.*

Gideon is on a mission. He is not satisfied with a partial victory; he goes after the full victory, even to the strongest of strongholds.

Gideon's response to the leaders of Succoth sounds harsh, but we have to understand what it says to us in type. It is says that it is possible to miss out! The people in Succoth and Penuel do not have faith in the future victory; therefore, they do not get to participate in it.

Judges 8:10-13 *Now Zebah and Zalmunna were at Karkor, and their armies with them, about fifteen thousand, all who were left of all the army of the people of the East; for one hundred and twenty thousand men who drew the sword had fallen.*

Then Gideon went up by the road of those who dwell in tents on the east of Nobah and Jogbehah; and he attacked the army while the camp felt secure. When Zebah and Zalmunna fled, he pursued them; and he took the two kings of Midian, Zebah and Zalmunna, and routed the whole army. Then Gideon the son of Joash returned from battle, from the Ascent of Heres.

In these verses, we learn that everything can change in one day when we go for the complete victory!

How The Enemy Truly Sees You

Judges 8:18 *And he said to Zebah and Zalmunna, "What kind of men were they whom you killed at Tabor?" So they answered, "As you [are], so were they; each one resembled the son of a king."*

Here is an insight into how the enemy sees us that we should not miss: the enemy sees us as children of a king!

The enemy sees us as royalty. He knows that we are children of the King. He is lying when he whispers that we are worthless or that we can't do it. Despite the tailor-made lies that the enemy throws at us, the Lord wants us to be so full of His Word that we can discern the lies of the enemy when we hear them.

Judges 8:19-21 *Then he said, "They were my brothers, the sons of my mother. As the Lord lives, if you had let them live, I would not kill you." And he said to Jether his firstborn, "Rise, kill them!" But the youth would not draw his sword; for he was afraid, because he was still a youth. So Zebah and Zalmunna said, "Rise yourself, and kill us; for as a man is, so is his strength." So Gideon arose and killed Zebah and Zalmunna, and took the crescent ornaments that were on their camels' necks.*

We are all in this together until the end. It is not for the fearful. It is not for the immature.

It's All For God's Glory

Philippians 3:14-15 *I press toward the goal for the prize of the upward call of God in Christ Jesus. Therefore let us, as many as are mature, have this mind; and if in anything you think otherwise, God will reveal even this to you.*

Judges 8:22-23 *Then the men of Israel said to Gideon, "Rule over us, both you and your son, and your grandson also; for you have delivered us from the hand of Midian." But Gideon said to them, "I will not rule over you, nor shall my son rule over you; the Lord shall rule over you."*

We are almost done with the story of Gideon, but there is one more very important lesson to learn. We must remember: if we are going to rise up to be who God has called us to be with valor and great victory, we must give all the glory to God. The victory is given to increase the domain of our King Jesus, not to create our own kingdom.

Judges 8:28 *Thus Midian was subdued before the children of Israel, so that they lifted their heads no more. And the country was quiet for forty years in the days of Gideon.*

Gideon changes a nation, but he starts out hiding in a winepress, threshing the wheat. He is living in a cave made by his own hands. If Gideon could come forth, if he could hear the word of the Lord say, "You mighty man of valor!", we can, too! We can rise up and know that the enemy himself sees us as children of the King. The Lord says, "Stand on the Word! Bring your food with you! Be a light to those around you! Blow your prophetic trumpet!" The Lord desires for us to be forerunners. He wants to eliminate our fears, if we would only allow Him.

May each of us stand in our God-ordained place and change the earth!

Make It Personal

1. Ask the Lord to help you identify times of spiritual warfare in your life when your identify and calling have been under siege. Identifying these seasons for what they are, and realizing the scheme in play, can bring increased clarity and even resolve.

2. There were tests Gideon needed to pass, tests that are necessary for us as well.
   - Has fear been cut out of my thinking to where it no longer has the final say? If not, where is there still a stronghold?
   - Am I confident (unwavering and resolved) in what God has called me to accomplish?
   - What is my relationship with the Word of God? Do I consume it daily and have an increase in spiritual vision?
   - God invites us into the battle for His Kingdom, and to share in the victories, but am I willing to give Him all the glory? Do I have a need to be recognized or applauded?

CHAPTER 7

Guess Who?!

I hope you are beginning to see how much your identity matters to the Kingdom, to the earth, and to yourself. At this point, I want to share what may be the most pivotal story in our entire study on identity. It is the story of Jonah.

John 8:32 *And you shall know the truth, and the truth shall make you free.*

John 8:36 *Therefore if the Son makes you free, you shall be free indeed.*

In John 8, Jesus is talking to some of His followers, and He tells them that the truth will make them free. Jesus Himself is the Truth. He is the Word made flesh. Therefore, if the Son makes you free, you shall be free indeed! The truth of the Word unlocks chains and pulls down strongholds. If we take hold of the truth of the Word, we will be out of the winepress, and we will be out of the cave!
Even as we started this study with the cry from the Book of Exodus, "Let my people go!", I believe that cry remains the heartbeat of God's people. There is a greater freedom coming to the people of God! May we be set free from the enemy's lies that have been spoken to us; may we be released from the confusion and fear that has been foisted on us!

I pray for the worldwide Body of Christ to experience a great freedom to be who we are called to be, becoming people who are ready to take hold of all that the Lord has placed before us.

Matthew 28:18-20 *And Jesus came and spoke to them, saying, "All authority has been given to Me in heaven and on earth. Go therefore and make disciples of all the nations, baptizing them in the name of the Father and of the Son and of the Holy Spirit, teaching them to observe all things that I have commanded you; and lo, I am with you always, [even] to the end of the age." Amen.*

Psalm 68:11 *The Lord gave the word; Great was the company of those who proclaimed it.*

Jonah's Great Call

I want to conclude this book by looking at the story of Jonah. Jonah is a prophet in the Bible who initially suffers from tremendous confusion, but who ultimately finds great freedom in a second chance.

Jonah 1:1 *Now the word of the LORD came to Jonah the son of Amittai, saying,*

Jonah's name means "dove," and his father's name, Amittai, means "my truth." Isn't it interesting that right at the beginning - even at Jonah's birth - we know the ingredients of his prophetic destiny? Jonah would need the Holy Spirit, represented in Scripture as the dove, as well as the truth of the Word to accomplish his purpose. We need the same two elements in our Kingdom lives!

Jonah 1:2 *Arise, go to Nineveh, that great city, and cry out against it; for their wickedness has come up before Me.*

We've seen such similar themes mirrored throughout these stories. There is always an "arise" that has to come. We also must rise up!

What an extraordinary call the Lord gives to Jonah! Nineveh is not a typical destination, for it is where their greatest enemy lives. How would a prophet like Jonah be able to accomplish such a mission? The answer is contained in the essence of who he is: dove, and son of my truth. The Holy Spirit and the Word could have enabled Jonah to fulfill his destiny in Nineveh right at the beginning...

But Jonah Goes Another Way!

Jonah 1:3 *But Jonah arose to flee to Tarshish from the presence of the Lord. He went down to Joppa, and found a ship going to Tarshish; so he paid the fare, and went down into it, to go with them to Tarshish from the presence of the Lord.*

But Jonah... Oh, if only we could see where our bad choices would take us, we wouldn't have so many unpleasant detours! Jonah has an unpleasant detour coming his way as soon as he flees from the presence of the Lord!

How interesting that the name Joppa means "beautiful." It reminds me of how Lot chooses to live in Sodom and Gomorrah because it looks good to him. How often we choose to go a different way because it looks more attractive.

Not only does Jonah choose to go a different way, he also has to pay a fare to go there. We are going to pay a price to fulfill the call of God on our lives, but we are also going to pay a price if we choose to not fulfill it! Jonah has to pay a price to go in the opposite direction, away from the presence of the Lord.

But God Has Another Plan!

Jonah 1:4 *But the Lord sent out a great wind on the sea, and there was a mighty tempest on the sea, so that the ship was about to be broken up.*

When we are heading in the wrong direction, everything can start to feel like it is coming apart. We thought we were heading in a better, "safer" direction, but when we are on the wrong ship, we are headed for shipwreck! We may not comprehend it at the beginning of the voyage, but we surely will along the way. We may think, "Hey, there's a big cruise boat; it's all good. I paid my price; this will end wonderfully." However, that will not be the case, and we won't be the first ones who notice. Like Abraham and Sarah, when they denied who they really were, the world recognized the disastrous ramifications first.

Jonah 1:5-6 *Then the mariners were afraid; and every man cried out to his god, and threw the cargo that was in the ship into the sea, to lighten the load. But Jonah had gone down into the lowest parts of the ship, had lain down, and was fast asleep. So the captain came to him, and said to him, "What do you mean, sleeper? Arise, call on your God; perhaps your God will consider us, so that we may not perish."*

Just like we saw before, the earth is crying out for us to take action! It is the ship's captain who has to go to the sleeping believer: the prophet Jonah. It is the captain who wakes Jonah up! The world is crying out for us to wake up and call on God, so that they not perish! Let us stir ourselves from slumber on this wrong-directioned ship and realize we can no longer sleep through the urgency of the hour.

We must wake up and realize that if we are not who we are supposed to be, then others are perishing.

Romans 13:11 *And do this, knowing the time, that now it is high time to awake out of sleep; for now our salvation is nearer than when we first believed.*

1 Thessalonians 5:6 *Therefore let us not sleep, as others do, but let us watch and be sober.*

The Lord has set the alarm clock, and it is ringing a resounding sound. There may be people slumbering all around you, but you need to wake up. As you wake up, others will sense the stirring of the atmosphere, and they will begin to rise as well. We must arise!

Jonah 1:7 *And they said to one another, "Come, let us cast lots, that we may know for whose cause this trouble has come upon us." So they cast lots, and the lot fell on Jonah.*

The people who are on the ship recognize that the situation is dire. They recognize it is not a typical voyage, and that they need supernatural help. They sense that the difficulties began due to someone's action, though the truth is the trouble came due to someone's inaction!

A Curious Inquisition!

Jonah 1:8 *Then they said to him, "Please tell us! For whose cause is this trouble upon us? What is your occupation? And where do you come from? What is your country? And of what people are you?"*

Often, the world stumbles upon the right questions. Jonah's shipmates ask him four questions, and I believe they are God-questions. We need to answer these questions today. What a curious inquisition! The boat is blowing apart, and it looks like they are all going to perish, but they ask him questions to get to the root of the problem that has so desperately impacted them.

These same questions are echoing in the atmosphere of the earth today because God wants us to know what our true identity is.

The First Question

The first question they ask Jonah is, "What is your occupation?" In other words, they are inquiring of Jonah what he is supposed to be doing. They understand that he must know.

2 Corinthians 4:7 *But we have this treasure in earthen vessels, that the excellence of the power may be of God and not of us.*

If we don't know what we are supposed to be doing, we will be doing everything. Or nothing. We will be here, and then we will be there. We will start one thing, and then we will start another thing, all while wondering why we fail to accomplish what we set out to do. We need to know what we are called by the Lord to do because it is only in that endeavor that we will find meaning, success, and anointing. The Lord has placed a treasure trove of gifts within our earthen vessels that He intends for use in our brilliantly crafted, God-ordained functions. "What is YOUR occupation?"

The Second Question

The second question now arrives to Jonah, "Where do you come from?" I believe the same question comes to us! Perhaps a better way to phrase it would be, "What have you been through?"

What we have been through is of great importance. Each one of us have been through unique, often difficult experiences. The Lord wants to use every bit of your life because it will resonate with people around you. It is just as we discovered with the story of Peter and John Mark. They used their hard-learned lessons to comfort and restore others who struggled with similar circumstances.

Each one of us have been through some troubles, obstacles, and conflicts that the Lord can redeem to make part of your powerful testimony. First, we must come to grips with, "Where do you come from?" It is no use sweeping it under the rug and pretending there have been no struggles. In recognizing where we come from, we begin to possess keys for breakthrough for other people on our "ship."

Some of the greatest gifts of healing are resident in people who have experienced trials of sickness and infirmity. The Scriptures tell us that Jesus healed many because He had compassion on them. When you have experienced illness firsthand, you have compassion for those who are walking through that valley, and you can be used greatly by God. "Where do YOU come from?"

2 Corinthians 3:17-18 *Now the Lord is the Spirit; and where the Spirit of the Lord is, there is liberty. But we all, with unveiled face, beholding as in a mirror the glory of the Lord, are being transformed into the same image from glory to glory, just as by the Spirit of the Lord.*

The Third Question

The next question that comes to Jonah is, "What is your country?" In other words, who is your King? Who is in control of your life? Are you letting the Midianites control you, or have you come to recognize, as Gideon did, that you are a son or daughter of the King of Kings?

It is a vital question for each one of us to answer. When we know that we are truly a part of the Kingdom of God, we can operate under supernatural conditions because Jesus is our King. Where the Spirit of the Lord is there is liberty!

There is no King like our King. He is the Creator Architect of all the earth. He is the God of supernatural miracles and holds all power in His hands. If God wants to, He can translate me like Phillip to help me accomplish His purposes. Remember the seven miracles of Jesus in the Gospel of John are intimately tied to who He is as revealed through His "I Am" statements. If we want to see great, miraculous demonstrations operating within our lives, we must first understand who our King is. "What is YOUR country?"

The Fourth Question

The final question asked of Jonah by his shipmates is, "Of what people are you?" Comprehending that we are not doing the work of the Kingdom all on our own is vital. We need to understand and appreciate the Body of Christ. Jesus' great prayer in John 17 focuses on the unity of His followers. It is critical that we receive other people in the Body of Christ and never diminish the importance of any member of Christ's Church.

Romans 8:19 *For the earnest expectation of the creation eagerly waits for the revealing of the sons of God.*

Realizing who we are becomes all the more important because the earth is truly waiting. The earth is not looking for a religious organization; it's looking for people who walk in all that the Lord has destined them to be and to do. We might still be confused over who we are, but God isn't confused. This is the season to understand what Jeremiah understood: God had the blueprint for his life from the beginning. The same is true for each one of us.

Philippians 2:13 *For it is God who works in you both to will and to do for His good pleasure.*

The Lord has equipped each one of us to do that which He has called us to do. He gives us the desire and the ability to do it. This is what we see in King David. David may have been overlooked by others, being the youngest of eight brothers, but he knows he is a giant killer. The Lord gives him the desire to face down Goliath, and He also equips him with the stone to do it.

Jonah 1:9-10 *So he said to them, "I am a Hebrew; and I fear the Lord, the God of heaven, who made the sea and the dry land." Then the men were exceedingly afraid, and said to him, "Why have you done this?" For the men knew that he fled from the presence of the Lord, because he had told them.*

Why Are You Doing This To Us?

The earth is crying out! If you aren't who you are supposed to be; if you are playing the sibling instead of the spouse; if you are busy going on a ship in the wrong direction; then, if you could tune in your ear, you would hear, "Why are you doing this to us?!"

There is such a great task ahead of you! The Kingdom purpose that you were born for is there for you to rise up and claim. Our progress in actualizing who we are called to be is not a small thing; it is enormous, as it affects the entire earth.

Jonah 1:15 *So they picked up Jonah and threw him into the sea, and the sea ceased from its raging.*

In the Scriptures, the sea speaks of humanity. When we walk in our Kingdom purpose and allow the Lord to throw us in the midst of people, the atmosphere calms and becomes conducive to bring in the lost. Our gifts and callings are designed to bring in the Harvest.

A Most Unusual Vehicle!

Jonah 1:17 *Now the Lord had prepared a great fish to swallow Jonah. And Jonah was in the belly of the fish three days and three nights.*

I love this image! God has a plan to deliver us to the proper Kingdom destination. It might involve a big, old, smelly fish, but He has a plan, and it will bring you to the location that you need to be. We cannot be afraid of the vehicle that the Lord chooses to accomplish His purpose. In Genesis, Joseph's processing in slavery and in prison prepare him for the fulfillment of the dream that the Lord had given him.

Jonah 2:1-2 *Then Jonah prayed to the Lord his God from the fish's belly. And he said: "I cried out to the Lord because of my affliction, And He answered me. Out of the belly of Sheol I cried, And You heard my voice."*

Have you been through a lot to get to where you find yourself today? Does it feel like the belly of hell at times? Know that there has been a great purpose in it. We cannot despise those things. We don't seek them out, but they come to us. These very difficult circumstances are used by God to prepare you for what is ahead.

Jonah 2:10 *So the LORD spoke to the fish, and it vomited Jonah onto dry land..*

God is in control of all of the components of your life, and He is guiding your destiny when we cry out to Him. It is then that He will put us exactly where we need to be!

A Second-Time Season!

Jonah 3:1-3 *Now the word of the Lord came to Jonah the second time, saying, "Arise, go to Nineveh, that great city, and preach to it the message that I tell you." So Jonah arose and went to Nineveh, according to the word of the Lord. Now Nineveh was an exceedingly great city, a three-day journey in extent.*

I prophetically sense that we are currently in a "second-time" season. It is an hour of restoration. It is a second-time opportunity to take back what the enemy may have stolen from you. There are many examples in the Scriptures to encourage us in this "second-time" season. Think about some of these. The 10 commandments came a second time after the terrible sin of the golden calf.

There are many examples in the Scriptures to encourage us in this "second-time" season. Think about some of these. The 10 commandments came a second time after the terrible sin of the golden calf. Israel failed to go into the Promised Land under Moses, but had a second successful opportunity under Joshua. Isaac was finally born after Ishmael. Samson had a second opportunity for victory after Delilah. Peter had a second chance after denying Jesus. The pattern is set throughout the Bible.

God is saying, "You can be different than you were before." That which defined you in the past doesn't need to define you in the future. I believe He is bringing your life into clarity, even if you've had a season when you were going in the wrong direction. If you pray, "Lord, I want another chance!", then this is the day! If you have previously said, "No!" to the Lord, go back to Him and say, "Yes!"

This is an hour of great opportunity! It's all-hands-on-deck! The Great Harvest is calling! It is what the Lord has ordained from the very beginning. It is an Esther hour! Who knows if you have come to the Kingdom for such an hour as this? Can you imagine that you have come to this place and this time - not as a mistake or as happenstance - as part of the very purposes of God? Let the Lord bring you into alignment with the blueprint He has had for you all along.

Make It Personal

1. Ask yourself the same four questions Jonah was asked.
    - What is your occupation? Or, What are you supposed to be doing?
    - Where do you come from? Or, What have you been through?
    - What is your country? Or, Who is your king? Who is in control of your life?
    - Of what people are you? Or, Who is working alongside you?

CHAPTER 8

I Did It On Purpose!

There is something I love about the month of January. I enjoy the concept of a New Year! It's a chance to reconfigure our lives. It's a chance to make life-changing adjustments. It's such a God-ordained opportunity. I believe we can have a New Year at any time! As you read this, <u>today</u> is one of those days!

As I conclude this book about identity, I want to address purpose: <u>your</u> purpose. I am calling this chapter "I Did It On Purpose!" because we must know our God-given purpose, and, if we are to see it come to pass, we must do it <u>on purpose</u>!

Philippians 3:12b...*that I may apprehend that for which also <u>I am apprehended of Christ Jesus.</u>*

You Have Been Created On Purpose With A Purpose!

The Lord created you on purpose with a purpose, and I want to encourage you to fulfill your purpose: to <u>do</u> your purpose <u>on</u> purpose!

Psalm 126:5-6 *Those who sow in tears <u>shall</u> reap in joy. He who <u>CONTINUALLY goes forth</u> weeping, bearing seed for sowing, <u>shall doubtless come again with rejoicing, bringing his sheaves with him</u>.*

What a great purpose God has given each one of us, but fulfilling our purpose isn't easy or automatic. In fact, we need to continually sow seeds into our purpose - often with difficulties and even weeping - but, in the end, it will bring you joy and great fruit!

We see it clearly in Jesus' life. In the week before Jesus' death, Jesus knew what awaited Him.

John 12:27 *Now My soul is troubled, and what shall I say? 'Father, save Me from this hour'? But for this purpose I came to this hour.*

The truth is that our purpose can propel us to accomplish and endure great difficulties, but we have to keep doing our purpose on purpose. We can't give up!

The Apostle Paul had a great purpose, but he also had prophecies telling him that he would suffer in the fulfilling of his purpose. Paul did indeed suffer. Let's look at what happened to him in Lystra:

Acts 14:8-10, 19-22 *And in Lystra a certain man without strength in his feet was sitting, a cripple from his mother's womb, who had never walked. This man heard Paul speaking. Paul, observing him intently and seeing that he had faith to be healed, said with a loud voice, "Stand up straight on your feet!" And he leaped and walked...Then Jews from Antioch and Iconium came there; and having persuaded the multitudes, they stoned Paul and dragged him out of the city, supposing him to be dead.*

However, when the disciples gathered around him, he rose up and went into the city. And the next day he departed with Barnabas to Derbe. And when (Barnabas and Paul) had preached the gospel to that city and made many disciples, they returned to Lystra, Iconium, and Antioch, strengthening the souls of the disciples, exhorting them to continue in the faith, and saying, "We must go through many tribulations enter the kingdom of God."

Many people would say that they want the great healing ministry that Paul had, but are they willing to also have the difficulties that accompany such a great call and purpose? If we want the dynamic, Spirit-filled destiny that the Lord intends, we must press through the tribulations. This is why we must do our purpose on purpose.

Jeremiah's Great Purpose

Let's look at the story of Jeremiah's great purpose, and how he fulfilled it on purpose. Many quote the well-known verse regarding Jeremiah's destiny found in Jeremiah 1:5. It's the verse about Jeremiah's profound purpose being ordained by God from the womb. Each one of us has a significant destiny from God that God ordained from the womb. What does it mean to have a meaningful purpose? What did it mean in Jeremiah's life? And what does it mean for our lives?

We can see the entirety of Jeremiah's call in Jeremiah 1:1-10. Let's take a look at it verse by verse.

Jeremiah 1:1 *The words of Jeremiah the son of Hilkiah, of the priests who were in Anathoth in the land of Benjamin,*

The name Jeremiah means "appointed of Jehovah." We, like Jeremiah, are appointed of Jehovah. Jeremiah's father's name is Hilkiah, which means "portion of Jehovah." We have each been given gifts from the Lord. They are the portion of God that we carry to help us supernaturally fulfill our purposes.
We also see that Jeremiah is of the priestly line. Like Jeremiah, we are also priests! That's what we read in 1 Peter 2:9.

1 Peter 2:9 *But you are a chosen generation, a royal priesthood, a holy nation, His own special people, that you may proclaim the praises of Him who called you out of darkness into His marvelous light;*

136

And Jeremiah comes from a place named Anathoth which means "answers to prayer." What a wonderful place to live! We also must live in a place of prayer, for there is an enemy - who is a thief and a liar - who will try to rob us of our purpose and our identity.

We learn that Anothoth iss in the land of Benjamin. Benjamin means "son of the right hand." If you have Jesus as your Lord, you have also been birthed as a child of the living God! Each of us are JUST LIKE JEREMIAH!

Jeremiah 1:2 *To whom the word of the LORD came in the days of Josiah the son of Amon, king of Judah, in the thirteenth year of his reign.*

Jeremiah's purpose stands in good times! Josiah is a good king, and life comes easily to Jeremiah at this point in his life.

Jeremiah 1:3 *It came also in the days of Jehoiakim The son of Josiah, king of Judah, until the end of the eleventh year of Zedekiah the son of Josiah, king of Judah, until the carrying away of Jerusalem captive in the fifth month.*

Jeremiah's Purpose Stood In Good Times And Bad

Jeremiah's purpose also stands in bad times! Jehoiakim and Zedekiah are bad kings whose reigns last for years. Your purpose and who the Lord has called you to be still stands, despite difficult circumstances and what can seem like a very long time.

Jeremiah 1:4-5
Then the word of the LORD came to me, saying:
Before I formed you in the womb I knew you; Before you were born I sanctified you; I ordained you a prophet to the nations.

The purpose the Lord places on you is not an afterthought! He knew the circumstances that Jeremiah was going to face. It is important to remember this truth during the difficult times.

Jeremiah 1:6 *Then said I: "Ah, Lord GOD! Behold, I cannot speak, for I am a youth."*

We may have all sorts of reasons that we feel disqualified for the purpose and identity that the Lord has given us. This is especially true during trying seasons. We must remember that it is the Lord who qualifies us!

1 Corinthians 1:1a *Paul, called to be an apostle of Jesus Christ <u>through the will of God</u>...*

Clearly, Paul could not have predicted that he would be the one to fulfill the call God places on him. He is the great persecutor of the Church until the Lord gets ahold of him in Acts 9! It is through this great encounter that Paul learns what his identity is. It's not our own doing, or our own call, or even our own identity; it is the one that the Lord created us for!

Jeremiah 1:7-9 <u>*But*</u> *the LORD said to me: "<u>Do not say</u>, 'I am a youth,' For <u>you SHALL go to ALL to WHOM I SEND YOU</u>, And whatever <u>I COMMAND YOU</u>, you <u>SHALL speak</u>. Do not be afraid of their faces, For I am with you to deliver you," says the Lord. Then the Lord put forth His hand and touched my mouth, and the Lord said to me: "Behold, <u>I have put My words in your mouth</u>.*

The Lord will give us what we need <u>if</u> we are willing. We must no longer say that the things of the Kingdom are for another. We must no longer say that they are not intended for us because they <u>are</u> intended for us!

Jeremiah 1:10 *See, <u>I have</u> this day set you over the nations and over the kingdoms, <u>To root out and to pull down</u>, <u>To destroy and to throw down</u>, <u>To build and to plant</u>."*

We have an identity and a ministry because we have a purpose. People are waiting for us. They're waiting for us to both pull down and to build. We must remember that it is the Lord who has set us in place. However, we can only accomplish it when we set out to do our purpose on purpose, for the enemy will try to prevent us at every turn. It doesn't come without battles.

1 Corinthians 16:9 *For a great and effective door has opened to me, and there are many adversaries.*

It is because of your purpose that you will have difficulties. They actually go hand in hand. We can't give up because of the difficulties, but we should rather receive them as a sign of encouragement.

The story of Jeremiah is that he is called to minister as a prophet to the nations. That is his identity. That is his great purpose. However, in his life, when times are difficult, Jeremiah is chained up, thrown into prison, put into a pit, and, many times, he barely escapes death. There is nothing about fulfilling his purpose that is automatic or easy for Jeremiah. In fact, this might give us some insight as to why Jeremiah is also known as "the weeping prophet!"

Jeremiah 9:1 *Oh, that my head were waters, And my eyes a fountain of tears, That I might weep day and night…*

Life is certainly not easy for Jeremiah, but he never gives up! Among many other things, Jeremiah is frequently in open conflict with the evil kings Jehoiakim and Zedekiah. When we look at the account in the Book of Jeremiah, we discover that Jeremiah continues to preach the words the Lord gives him, even though it isn't easy.

It is because of his unwanted preaching that Jeremiah is officially banned by the king from public appearances. That is most certainly a tough blow for someone called to be a preacher!

Jeremiah therefore writes his messages to be read by his assistant, Baruch. Jeremiah is going to accomplish his purpose NO MATTER WHAT comes his way. Jeremiah ends up having to write the same message three times because it keeps getting destroyed. The wicked King Jehoiakim even burns his manuscript. Let's look at the story in Jeremiah 36 because I think it will encourage you that you can also keep pressing forward with who God has made you to be!

The Word Comes To Jeremiah, But The King Doesn't Like It!

Jeremiah 36:1-4 *Now it came to pass in the fourth year of Jehoiakim the son of Josiah, king of Judah, that this word came to Jeremiah from the Lord, saying: Take a scroll of a book and write on it all the words that I have spoken to you against Israel, against Judah, and against all the nations, from the day I spoke to you, from the days of Josiah even to this day. It MAY be that the house of Judah will hear all the adversities which I purpose to bring upon them, that everyone MAY turn from his evil way, that I MAY forgive their iniquity and their sin.*

Then Jeremiah called Baruch the son of Neriah; and Baruch wrote on a scroll of a book, at the instruction of Jeremiah, ALL the words of the LORD which He had spoken to him.

Let's look at the king's response once Jeremiah has done all that the Lord requested him to do.

Jeremiah 36:22-28 *Now the king was sitting in the winter house in the ninth month, <u>with a fire burning on the hearth before him</u>. And it happened, when Jehudi had read three or four columns (Of Jeremiah's scroll that Baruch wrote), that <u>the king cut it with the scribe's knife and cast it into the fire that was on the hearth, until all the scroll was consumed in the fire that was on the hearth</u>....Now after the king had burned the scroll with the words which Baruch had written at the instruction of Jeremiah, the word of the LORD came to Jeremiah, saying: <u>Take yet another scroll</u>, and <u>write on it all the former words that were in the first scroll which Jehoiakim the king of Judah has burned</u>.*

It Isn't Just The King

Who Doesn't Like Jeremiah!

Jeremiah's purpose from the Lord still stands, despite the discouraging response. It isn't just the King who persecutes Jeremiah. Jeremiah is persecuted by:

His own family.

Jeremiah 12:6 *For <u>even your brothers</u>, the house of your father, Even they have dealt treacherously with you; Yes, <u>they have called a multitude after you</u>. <u>Do not believe them</u>, Even though they speak smooth words to you.*

His town of Anathoth

Jeremiah 11:21-22a *Therefore thus says the LORD concerning the men of Anathoth <u>who seek your life</u>, saying, 'Do not prophesy in the name of the LORD, lest you die by our hand'--therefore thus says the LORD of hosts: 'Behold, I will punish them...*

Jeremiah is also persecuted by the entire nation of Judah, a false prophet by the name of Hananiah, and much of the religious world.

Not only is Jeremiah persecuted for his messages, the Lord also asks him to remain unmarried.

Jeremiah 16:1-2 *The word of the Lord also came to me, saying, <u>You shall not take a wife, nor shall you have sons or daughters</u>...*

Ultimately, despite discouragement and loneliness, Jeremiah fulfills his purpose on purpose!

Jeremiah 20:7-9O *Lord, <u>You induced me, and I was persuaded; You are stronger than I, and have prevailed</u>. I am <u>in derision daily</u>; Everyone mocks me. For when I spoke, I cried out; I shouted, "Violence and plunder!" Because the word of the LORD was made to me a reproach and a derision daily. Then I said, "I will not make mention of Him, Nor speak anymore in His name." <u>But His word was in my heart like a burning fire shut up in my bones; I was WEARY of holding it back, And I could not</u>.*

Your Purpose Is A Fire In Your Bones!

That which the Lord has called you to do and to be rests as a fire in your bones! Do not hold it back! God's purpose in your life stands.

Jeremiah 29:11 *For <u>I know the thoughts that I think toward you</u>, says the Lord, thoughts of peace and not of evil, <u>to give you a future and a hope</u>.*

Your God-given purpose gives you a future and a hope! In Jeremiah 32, we see that, while Jeremiah is in prison, he is commanded by God to buy a field in Anothoth from his cousin Hanamel. This illustrates that, in spite of the advancing Babylonian enemy armies that were taking the land, everything would change again.

142

If you are going through difficulties, things WILL change again IF you don't give up!

Jeremiah 32:15 *Houses and fields and vineyards shall be possessed again in this land!*

They will be possessed again in this land of Anothoth - this land of answered prayers!

There are times you have to buy into your purpose even when no one else sees the value. The place that you buy it is in the land of answered prayer.

Nothing Is Too Hard For God!

After Jeremiah buys the land, he makes a great proclamation:

Jeremiah 32:17 *Ah, Lord God! Behold, You have made the heavens and the earth by Your great power and outstretched arm. There is nothing too hard for You.*

This is what I proclaim to you today! There is NOTHING too hard for the Lord. If He has called you, He will THEREFORE enable you!

Philippians 2:13 *For it is God who works in you both to will and to do for His good pleasure.*

God does both! He gives us both the will AND the ability to do.

Jeremiah 33:3 *Call to Me, and I WILL answer you, and show you great and mighty things, which you do not know.'*

Remember: having a clear identity and purpose does not mean that it is easy. We saw that in Jesus' life, Paul's life, and now in Jeremiah's life. They were people of purpose, and yet they also had to sow some tears. They accomplished their purposes on purpose because they didn't give up, no matter how difficult the struggle.

Galatians 6:9 *And LET US not be weary in well doing: for in due season we shall reap, if we faint not.*

Romans 8:28 *And we know that all things work together for good to those who love God, to those who are the called according to HIS PURPOSE.*

Let us remember that it is going to take some determination on our parts.

Matthew 11:12 *And from the days of John the Baptist until now the kingdom of heaven suffers violence, and the violent take it by force.*

Let our cry be "I did it on purpose!" We may sow some tears in the process, but we will be certain to reap in joy and bring our sheaves with us!

Make It Personal

1. If there is yet uncertainty about what your purpose is, consider these two questions: What makes you cry? What makes you bang your fist on the table? In other words, what stirs the deepest emotion in you? What are you not okay with, if it were to stay the same as it is today? You must do something about it – like Jeremiah, it is like a fire in your bones!

2. What price are you willing to pay for your answer to the above question? There will likely be financial, relational, emotional, physical and spiritual costs involved. Sometimes, tremendous costs (2 Corinthians 11:16-29).

3. According to Hebrews 12:20, what compelled Jesus? What hope did Paul have at the end of his life (2 Timothy 4:6-8)? Read again the verses included in the last subsection of this chapter, Nothing Is Too Hard For God! Now what will you resolve to do, according to the power of the Holy Spirit working in you?

EPILOGUE

I can't end this book without praying for you! Oh, I have such an excitement in my spirit for what the Lord wants to do. The Lord has brought you to the Kingdom for such a time as this. He has formed you, given you gifts and experiences, and watched over you to have you come forth in the identity that He intended all along. It's powerful! Lord Jesus, I ask for You to touch each one. Lord, I pray that You would rise up in each one and that they would say, "I will arise!" Lord God, let each one blow their prophetic trumpets. Let each one consume Your Word. Cause them to take the double portion of the manna, that they would consume it, and that there would be enough for them. As they themselves eat the fat and drink the sweet, may they prepare portions for whom nothing has been prepared. Lord God, I pray that each one reading this book would be released to be exactly what Your blueprint for them had in mind. Lord, I pray that all fear in their lives would be highlighted and that they would recognize when it's fear, and Lord, that it would be separated from them completely. Lord, may we be strong and courageous, as we read in the admonition in Joshua to the children of Israel. Let us be strong and very courageous. Let us not look at things and say, "Oh, I don't know if we can do it," but instead, may we have the spirit of David within us. Lord, let us say, "How dare you, you uncircumcised enemy; how dare you defy the armies of the living God?!" Lord, I pray over the destiny of every single one praying this prayer. Lord, let not one thing fall to the ground. Lord, Your purposes are right. Oh God, cause us to be those who would walk in everything You have called us to. May we take our place, Lord God: the place that You have ordained, and we would not be afraid to be exactly who You have called us to be. Lord, I pray that You would bless each one. In Jesus' Name, amen.

AUTHOR'S BIOGRAPHY

Dr. Nina Baratiak

ninabaratiak@gmail.com

Raised in a Jewish home, Dr. Nina Baratiak had a miraculous encounter with Jesus on Halloween, 1976 leading her to accept Him as her Messiah. From that point forward, Nina has had a vision to see the Church realize its full potential as an effective demonstration of Christ's love and power to all corners of the earth. Nina has been a sought after teacher and preacher for over 30 years and has been given opportunities, both in the United States and abroad, to share the message God has placed on her heart: to see each person set free and established to live completely for Jesus. Nina is known for teaching the whole Bible while preaching a unique word and developing classes that are fresh and anointed. Nina's vision every time she shares the Word is that the substance of her message embraces a prophetic significance for the hour that we live in and that everyone would receive a powerful impartation in order to enable them to walk fully in their destiny. Nina and her husband John live in the San Francisco Bay area and are on the Pastoral Team at Shiloh Church Oakland.